What people have sai[d about] Mike Baxter's previous books

Reviews of The Strategy Manual

"Best management book I've read all year."

"Highly actionable, well-referenced and a pleasure to follow. In my opinion, it does everything a business book should do but rarely does."

"Highly informative and easy to put into practice."

"Very useful and practical models that I am able to use straight away with clients in strategy work."

"As a seasoned practitioner, who's worked with an enviable roster of clients, there's no theory here - he's making the mental models and methodologies that you'd normally expect from tier-one management consultancies available to everyone."

Review of Core Values

"Essential reading for any organisation that's reviewing its vision statement."

Review of University Strategy 2020

"This report will be of great value to university leaders and their advisers. At times it will be uncomfortable reading because it has a ruthless focus on what is important in good strategy."

AI-Augmented Decisions:
A Practical Guide

Helping you make better, smarter, faster
decisions using generative AI platforms

Mike Baxter

Goal Atlas Ltd

First published by Goal Atlas Ltd, Isleworth, UK.

British Library Cataloguing-in-Publication Data: A catalogue record for
this book is available from the British Library.

ISBN: 978-1-9191865-0-4

Cover image from Midjourney

Dedicated to the memory of Professor Maggie Boden OBE

1936 – 2025

The "Godmother of AI" and a formative influence during
my undergraduate years at the University of Sussex

Contents

Disclaimer

It is the central premise of this book that AI is now capable of usefully and valuably augmenting human decision-making for high-impact, high-complexity decisions.

The important disclaimer, however, is that this book is all about using AI to enable humans to make faster, smarter, better decisions, not for AI to make the decisions on our behalf.

DECISION-MAKING IS ALWAYS THE RESPONSIBILITY OF HUMANS. AIs MAKE ASSUMPTIONS AND MISTAKES – ALWAYS DOUBLE CHECK THEIR RESPONSES.

The use of AI tools can also introduce new types of data security issues, not necessarily raised by other types of technology. Before using any of the AI techniques described in this book, please make sure you are acting in compliance with your own organisation's AI policies and standards. If you don't have any such policies and standards, guidance on data and security issues can be found from the National Cyber-Security Centre in the USA[1] or from the Information Commissioner's Office in the UK.[2]

About Mike Baxter

Dr Mike Baxter has been awarded a PhD in Science, a personal Professorship and Chartered Designer status. He has been a business consultant since 2001, delivering well over 10,000 hours of consultancy to the leadership of some of the world's biggest brands, including Cisco, Google, HSBC, Lilly, Sony PlayStation and Skype. With a background in psychology, design and higher education, he has been an advisor and facilitator to global businesses, the UK government, vice-chancellors and the leadership teams of UK universities and to some of London's fastest growing tech start-ups. Mike is a recognised specialist in the field of strategy and strategic thinking and is the author of several books, including 'The Strategy Manual', 'Core Values' and 'Deep Design Thinking'.

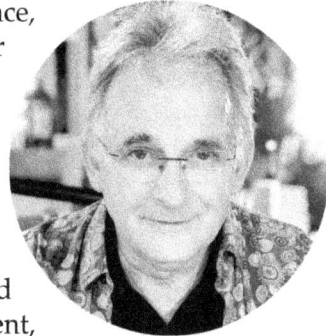

Mike's company, Goal Atlas Ltd,[3] was established in 2014 to work with leaders and teams, across sectors, to facilitate high-complexity, high-impact decisions and secure their adoption. Goal Atlas undertakes consultancy and independent research into AI, strategy and decision-making and offers models and frameworks to make these impactful within organisations.

These are some of the organisations Mike has worked with…

CHAPTER 1: About this book, why you need it and how it works

What is this book about?

Do you find yourself having to make high-stakes decisions in an increasingly complex world? Are you, perhaps, trying to evolve your workforce, transform your services or expand into new sectors or markets? Have you also been wondering for some time now just how AI is going to make a real difference to your own ways of working? If so, this is the book for you!

Who is this guide for?

This guide is designed for decision-makers who need to navigate high-impact, high-complexity choices in today's fast-moving environment:

- **Senior Business Leaders** - CEOs, directors and department heads making strategic decisions about growth, transformation, market positioning or operational changes that will shape their organisation's future. If you're dealing with decisions where the stakes are high, the variables are numerous and traditional analysis feels insufficient, this book will help you cut through complexity to make faster, smarter, better decisions.

- **Non-Profit and Public Sector Leaders** - Executive directors, program managers and policy makers evolving services, operations or strategic direction while balancing diverse stakeholder needs, limited resources and complex social outcomes. This book will help you maintain mission alignment while making pragmatic decisions about resource allocation and service delivery.

- **'Big' Decision-Makers** - Anyone responsible for 'big' decisions (i.e. high-impact, high-complexity decisions) that require coordination across multiple teams, involve significant uncertainty or demand integration of diverse perspectives and expertise. Whether you're managing a major project, implementing new technologies or restructuring operations, this book provides structure for decisions that traditional approaches struggle to handle effectively.

This guide focuses specifically on high-impact, high-complexity decisions rather than routine operational choices or simple either/or decisions that can be resolved through standard analytical approaches. If you're looking for help with day-to-day management decisions or straightforward cost-benefit analyses, you may find more targeted resources elsewhere. This book is for leaders who recognise that their most important decisions require a more sophisticated, systematic approach that can handle complexity whilst maintaining momentum towards action.

Why do you need this book?

In order to stay focused, remain effective and avoid falling behind their peers, organisations are having to make decisions that are harder than they used to be, and they need to make these decisions faster. Why? Well, here's what the research says:

> "A synthesis of multidisciplinary research reveals substantial evidence that modern organizations operate under significantly greater complexity than in previous decades, driven by systemic shifts in economic structures, technological proliferation, and socio-political dynamics." [4]

> "Empirical evidence from longitudinal studies, industry benchmarks, and behavioural research demonstrates that decision velocity has become a critical determinant of organizational success, with faster decisions correlating strongly with financial outperformance, operational agility, and strategic resilience." [5]

In other words, the work you do in your organisation probably requires you to make faster decisions in a more complex environment than at any time in the past.

To make faster, smarter, better decisions we need to solve the following decision-making problems:

- **Information overload:** We need to learn how to cut through overwhelming data to focus on what matters;

- **Decision complexity:** We need to develop a structured approach for tackling decisions with multiple stakeholders and far-reaching implications;

- **Cognitive biases:** We need to discover how to challenge assumptions and avoid common decision-making traps;

- **Implementation challenges:** We need to understand how to move from decision to action with clear validation and formalisation steps.

What practical value will this book deliver?

This book is designed to do two jobs:

1. Give you a **process** for making faster, smarter, better decisions. This process has been designed around key principles established from decades of decision science, complexity theory and behavioural economics.[6]

2. Give you **tools and prompts** to enable high-impact, high-complexity decisions to be augmented by artificial intelligence.

Once it has done these jobs, you will be able to:

- Clarify precisely what decision you need to make and why (and secure agreement on this with other key decision-makers) at the start of the decision-making process;

- Uncover patterns and insights to inform and enrich your decision-making;

- Run focused & structured decision-making workshops that lead to clear decision proposals;

- Test and validate your proposed decision before finally committing to it;

- Enable the decision to be adopted across the organisation and deliver its intended impact.

What makes this book different?

This book is a practical guide to get you making decisions in a more structured and systematic way and to get you using AI in a fully engaged, practical way to augment those decisions. The practicalities in this book derive from well over 10,000 hours of my strategy consultancy with leading brands, high-growth startups and transformative charities[7] and several decades of studying and applying AI – from Professor Maggie Boden's[8] pioneering courses on AI, while I was an undergraduate at the University of Sussex, to working with AI start-ups in London.[9]

AI-Augmented Decisions cuts through the AI hype to deliver immediate hands-on value. No prior AI experience is needed - from choosing and setting up your AI platform to crafting effective prompts, this guide takes you, step-by-step, through a robust, repeatable decision-making process. The book is designed to give you everything you need to start making faster, smarter, better decisions straight away, including five **free downloadable 'super-prompts'** to enable your decisions to be immediately augmented by the AI of your choice.

Making the best use of the rest of this book

Chapter 2 makes the case for improving the decision-making processes within your organisation, especially for high-impact, high-complexity decisions.

Chapter 3 walks you through the five-phase decision-making process that this book is built around: i) **Decision Scoping**, ii) **Decision Preparation**, iii) **Decision-Making Workshop**, iv) **Decision Validation** and v) **Decision Adoption**. It also explains where these five phases came from and why they provide a great foundation for your organisation's decision-making.

Chapter 4 explains why now is the moment to start AI-augmenting your decisions and then provides a simple guide to getting started with AI platforms.

Then Chapters 5 to 9 walk you through the five phases of best-practice decision-making, providing 'super-prompts' for you to use directly in your chosen AI platform, applied to the big decision that *you* want to make.

The case study: choosing the holiday of a lifetime

An important part of this book is the case study that is developed across all of the main process-focused chapters (Chapter 5 to 9). This case study focuses on 'choosing the holiday of a lifetime'. I chose this example as it is a high-impact (for the people involved) and high complexity decision yet is intuitive to follow and requires no particular business or specialist expertise. Using the 'super-prompts' from each chapter, I scope out my own 'holiday of a lifetime' and prepare for decision-making by researching alternative options and choosing selection criteria. Then I choose a particular holiday, validate my choice and set out all that needs to be done to make it happen.

For you, the reader, this gives you a tangible example of the principles of decision-making applied to a real-world decision. Between this case study and the downloads you can access for free, you will be able to see every prompt and every response from the AI that leads from an exploration of what a 'holiday of a lifetime' means for me, all the way to the practical details of how I make sure I've booked the right travel insurance for my chosen holiday. My main intention is to give you a fully worked case study to follow as you read the chapters and try out your own first AI-augmented decisions. You could also, if you want, work through your own 'choosing the holiday of a lifetime' decision and compare your process and outcomes with mine. This can be a gentle soft-landing into the world of AI-augmented decisions before diving into any real-world organisational decisions.

For me, the author, the case study gave me an end-to-end stress-test of my AI-augmented decision-making process. This enabled me to check that my super-prompts could cope with this, along with the dozens of real-world business and organisational decisions that I threw at it during the writing process.

Where this book sets out to innovate

Whilst this book is a practical guide to AI-augmenting a particular domain of knowledge (high-impact, high-complexity decision-making), it became increasingly obvious, as my writing progressed, that I was exploring the relatively new intellectual territory of 'how to produce representations of domains of human knowledge that are AI-legible and AI-actionable.'

I felt this was 'relatively new intellectual territory' for several reasons:

- When I started to write this book (late December 2024), most people writing about the practicalities of using AI were focused on how best to prompt AIs and to contextualise those prompts to exploit the *AI's own native expertise*; expertise gained from tens of terabytes of training data and manifested in trillion-parameter foundational models.[10]

- The few people that were trying to bestow AIs with domains of human knowledge, were doing so by producing custom GPTs (Generative Pre-trained Transformers).[11] A custom GPT fine-tunes an already powerful foundational model to understand and apply a domain of knowledge specific to your industry, company or even yourself. The issue with this is transparency.[12] Go to OpenAI's GPT store,[13] where any OpenAI user can create and publish their own Custom GPT and click on one of the featured GPTs. You will be presented with a title, a brief description and a few 'conversation starters'. The rulebook of custom instructions is hidden, the library of uploaded files providing context is secret and the actions enabling the GPT to interact with external APIs remains invisible. Unless you built the custom GPT yourself, its knowledge is very 'black box'.

- Of course, it could be argued that the foundational models underpinning Google's Gemini, Anthropic's Claude and OpenAI's GPT are representations of human knowledge in AI-legible, AI actionable ways. There are, therefore, thousands of computer scientists for which this is not new intellectual territory. But since I have neither the capability nor inclination to work on foundational models, my claim to novelty applies only to professional consumers of AI services, like me.

Over the past five years, I've written four books that set out to distil specific domains of knowledge. In *The Strategy Manual*,[14] for example, I offered a practical, good-practice framework for managing the full strategy lifecycle from production through adoption to adaptation. In my book *Core Values*,[15] I provided both a framework for thinking about the core values of organisations and a workflow for selecting those values and then applying them meaningfully to inspire and regulate that organisation.

As my plan for this book developed, I settled on a goal to guide my writing:

To make a domain of knowledge

legible to and actionable by AI

in a transparent, generalisable way.

I quickly settled on high-impact, high-complexity decision-making as my chosen 'domain of knowledge'. This is something a great many organisations struggle with. They struggle with strategy and strategic planning. They struggle with branding. They struggle with digital transformation. They struggle with crisis management. This is also a domain of knowledge where I had served a long apprenticeship. My 10,000+ hours of consultancy began in the fledgling e-commerce industry, moved on to digital transformation and, lately, has settled in organisational strategy.

To enable AI to augment humans in high-impact, high-complexity decisions, I first needed to distil the process humans themselves use for high-impact, high-complexity decisions. For reasons we will explore in depth in Chapter 3, I ended up with a five-phase process. For each of these phases, I then wrote a detailed 'super-prompt'. This is what makes the domain of knowledge legible to AI and actionable by AI, and it does so in a completely transparent way. The five-phase process is fully explained. The super-prompts are available for humans to read in order to understand what the AI is being asked to do and what context it is given for doing so. It is exactly this human-readable super-prompt that is uploaded to the AI and this is all the instruction and context the AI is given to supplement and focus its own foundation model.[16]

These super-prompts are also designed to be as generalisable as possible within the domain of expertise they are intended to operate in. In other words, I have written them and tested them to try to be as applicable to choosing a holiday of a lifetime as they are to deciding the strategy for a large business organisation.

These modest innovations are, I believe, the early forays into a huge world of opportunity to capture business value at scale from AI. In a few years' time, I foresee most organisations setting out to make their own proprietary domains of expertise legible and actionable by AI in a transparent and generalisable way.

How I did and didn't use AI in this book

Writing this book was itself an exercise in AI-augmented decision-making, a partnership that revealed as much about AI's incredible strengths as it did about its current critical limitations. It quickly became clear that while AI could not write this book, the book could not have been written without it. The problem is what I have labelled 'credible slop'. When suitably prompted, an AI will write something which, at first glance, seems perfectly readable and, at least to some extent, meaningful. However, try to draw a conceptual diagram of what it wrote and you'll find pieces missing. Try to apply any process it devised and you'll find flaws in its logic. It has made me realise that an important part of my job as a writer of books like this one is to get into the head of my readers and help you work your way through a challenge you might struggle with. The current generation of AIs don't do well in getting inside human heads and helping them think better. This is because they have been trained to understand human language but not the neuro-symbolic reasoning that underpins that language.[17]

So this book wasn't written by an AI. None of its chapters were written by an AI. But I cannot really say that none of its sentences were written by an AI. To explain why, we need to start exploring what AI is actually good at.

AI is currently astonishingly good at certain types of research: research that I'd characterise as shallow but broad. I begin the next chapter, for example, with the claim that companies don't survive for as long as they used to. This is a great issue to explore using 'deep research',[18] because it needs to find where this has been claimed on websites, business articles or blog posts and then check the sources they cite in support of those claims. Such research will produce a broad range of initial sources but the primary research is likely to be only one or two clicks away from those initial sources. All the deep research for this book has been done on either Gemini[19] or Perplexity.[20] Indeed, several of the references I cite are links to deep research queries and by clicking the URL provided you can even see how I undertook the research.

AI is also great at assimilating information from huge amounts of text. I, for example, was able to give Gemini the entirety of two of my previous books and get it to find everything related to the divergent / convergent cycles of design thinking (from my 102-page book *Deep Design Thinking*)[21] and suggest how they could be applied to high-impact, high-complexity decision-making (from my 431-page book *The Strategy Manual*).[22]

With lots of prompting and quite a bit of back-and-forth conversation, AI can be persuaded to do a good job of joining together fragments of information, sketched-out ideas and research findings into a readable narrative. We need to be acutely aware of the risk of credible slop here but AI can, at the very least, provide a thoughtful provocation for a new chunk of a chapter for me to re-write.

Finally, AI is brilliant at both critiquing material that I have written (given a framework on which to base the critique and stern instructions to actually be critical) and offering edits to increase readability or to get all the Chapter summaries written in the same voice and following a similar structure and style. In many ways, the process of writing this book mirrored the five-phase decision framework that this book is built around, with AI acting as a key augmenting partner at every stage:

1. Which bit of the book am I working on (decision-scoping)?
2. What do I need to know in order to write this bit of the book (decision

preparation)?

3. How do I draft this bit of the book (decision-making workshop)?

4. How do I check whether my draft is good enough (decision validation)?

5. How do I integrate what I've just written into the rest of the book (decision adoption)?

Needless to say, I got lots of help from AIs when writing the super-prompts – AIs were, after all, the intended consumers of those super-prompts so it would have been odd not to have sought their views.

This therefore is a book written by me, containing ideas that I synthesised far more from the work of other humans, on whose shoulders I stood, than from any AI. My writing has, however, been unashamedly AI-augmented, as indeed I suggest your high-impact, high-complexity decision-making should be.

CHAPTER 2: Why you need to improve your decision-making

This chapter aims to build a persuasive case for taking a structured, systematic, evidence-based approach to decision-making in your organisation, to ensure you make faster, smarter, better decisions ... but let's begin with a cautionary tale...

What can go wrong

There is clear evidence that companies don't survive as long as they used to.

> "The corporate world has undergone a profound transformation over the past century, with one of the most striking trends being the dramatically shortened lifespan of companies. What was once a landscape dominated by century-old industrial titans has evolved into a dynamic ecosystem where corporate survival beyond a few decades has become increasingly rare [...]
>
> Research from McKinsey & Company [found] that the average lifespan of S&P 500 companies was 61 years in 1958, but had plummeted to less than 18 years by 2016. Their analysis further predicted that by 2027, approximately 75% of the companies listed on the S&P 500 in 2016 will have disappeared through acquisitions, mergers, or bankruptcies."[23]

As the last part of this quote suggests, this dramatic fall in corporate longevity isn't necessarily always bad. Companies can merge or simply change their corporate identity and continue to flourish. Many, however, don't.

The tragedy of Kodak

The story of Kodak's response to digital photography represents one of the most instructive examples of an organisation failing to make key business decisions. What makes it particularly fascinating is that Kodak wasn't blindsided by the digital technology that eventually destroyed them - they invented it! In 1975, Kodak engineer Steven Sasson created the first digital camera.[24] Yet within three decades the company would file for bankruptcy having failed to adapt to the very technology they pioneered.

The root of this failure lies in the complex interplay between organisational structure, culture and decision-making processes. Kodak's organisational structure was built around its traditional film business, with chemical engineers dominating leadership positions in the company and a culture deeply rooted in the precision manufacturing of photographic materials. This structure created a form of institutional myopia - the organisation tended to see opportunities through the lens of its existing business model.

This myopia manifested in a series of fateful decisions. When confronted with digital technology, Kodak's leaders recognised that digital technology would destroy the 'moat' that had afforded them market leadership and strong profitability.[25] Photography would no longer depend on high levels of chemical engineering expertise and capital-intensive factories to produce and develop film. Instead, digital cameras required only a few specialised components (e.g. CCD sensor and memory chips) that could be sourced readily on the open market. They viewed digital as a threat to be managed rather than an opportunity to be seized.

The contrast with Fujifilm, Kodak's traditional competitor, is illuminating. Faced with the same disruption, Fujifilm diversified aggressively, leveraging its chemical expertise to enter new markets from cosmetics to pharmaceuticals.

The financial impact of Kodak's decisions was catastrophic.[26] From a position of market dominance in 1999, when the company generated $2.5 billion in profit,[27] Kodak suffered a dramatic decline to bankruptcy 13 years later. While they initially maintained revenue levels by shifting to digital cameras - even achieving 21.3% market share in the US in 2005 - this transition was financially disastrous. The company lost an estimated $60 for every digital camera sold in 2001, and their global market share plummeted from 27% in 1999 to just 7% by 2010. In 2011, the digital camera division lost $349 million, while their traditional film business generated only $34 million, marking the end of what had once been one of America's most innovative companies.

The lesson to be learned

The lesson to be learned, both from the decline in overall corporate longevity and from Kodak in particular, is that no matter how big or successful your organisation is right now, its continued success, and indeed its very survival, may be more precarious than you think. The challenges you face as an organisation are many and varied but what will seal your fate is not those challenges on their own as much as your response to them. And this all comes down to how well your organisation is able to make critical decisions.

The challenges facing decision-makers

There are many different challenges facing decision-makers within organisations and even the most experienced leaders and managers can fall prey to common decision-making pitfalls. Cognitive biases lead us to seek only the evidence that confirms our beliefs while dismissing contradictory information. 'Groupthink'[28] can emerge in teams, particularly when facing high-stakes decisions under time pressure. Many organisations struggle with 'premature convergence' - rushing to solutions before fully exploring alternatives. [29]

Furthermore, the sheer volume of data has become overwhelming, with 72% of business leaders reporting that data overload has actually prevented them from making decisions at times.[30] The decision-making landscape has also become more crowded and intricate – a 2022 survey of 1,100 UK senior business leaders, for example, found that, in 94% of cases, more than six people are involved in purchase-decision-making processes.[31] Meanwhile, the interconnected nature of modern business systems means that decisions have broader and faster-rippling consequences throughout organisations. Technology, while providing powerful tools, has added its own layer of complexity - organisations now manage between 250 (average across organisations) and 650 (large organisations) different software applications.[32] Perhaps unsurprisingly, 90% of workers report information overload as a major challenge.[33] The traditional tools and frameworks for decision-making, whilst still valuable, are increasingly insufficient for navigating this complex environment.

Different types of decision

Decisions are made all the time within organisations, but they vary considerably in both their impact and their complexity (Fig 1.).

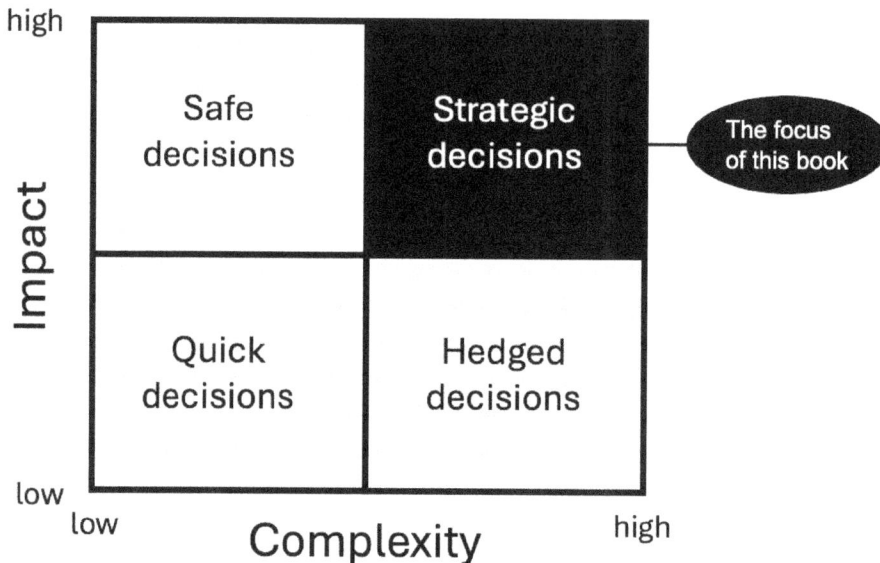

Figure 1 Different types of decisions need to be made in different ways

Low impact, low complexity decisions are the ones you don't want to spend too much time on. You want to decide quickly and move on. These can be considered 'quick decisions' because their low complexity means your rapidly-made decisions ought to be right a lot of the time, but, because they are also low impact, it doesn't matter that much if you get a few wrong. There are typically a great many of these types of decisions to be made within organisations – for many leaders and managers, they will be a daily, if not hourly, occurrence.

High impact, low complexity decisions have to be good decisions and should, as far as possible, lead to valuable outcomes. Their low complexity suggests that, with the right data and insights, these outcomes should be predictable. Hence the effort should be invested in getting good evidence, following the numbers and making 'safe decisions'.

Low impact, high complexity decisions live in the zone of experimentation. Outcomes will not always be predictable, even with the best data and insights. That's the nature of complexity. So, a test and learn approach that makes lots of 'hedged decisions' is the secret here. This aims to squeeze wins from a variety of potential outcomes.

High impact, high complexity decisions are decisions with strategic significance. They are the drivers of organisational transformation. They matter a lot, so it is important to invest time and effort to maximise their value. Their complexity, however, makes them especially difficult decisions, with no right or wrong answers, just better or worse ones.

Why focus on high-impact, high-complexity decisions?

While all four decision types can benefit from AI augmentation, strategic decisions (high-impact, high-complexity) represent the frontier where organisations have the most to gain and where guidance is most needed. Here's why:

1. **Highest organisational value:** Strategic decisions determine an organisation's future trajectory and how it prepares itself for challenges ahead. Getting these decisions right—or wrong—can mean the difference between industry leadership and obsolescence, as the Kodak example powerfully illustrates.

2. **Greatest augmentation potential:** While quick, safe and hedged decisions benefit from AI primarily through automation and information processing (which are increasingly well-understood), strategic decisions can involve nuanced human-AI collaboration where frameworks and methodologies are still emerging.

3. **Less commoditised guidance:** AI applications for quick, safe and hedged decisions tend toward more procedural challenges—dashboard creation, database integration, experiment design—which are already well-documented in technical literature. Strategic decision augmentation, by contrast, lacks established frameworks and best practices.

4. **More challenging human-AI integration:** Strategic decisions require sophisticated integration of human judgment with AI capabilities, raising questions about how to structure prompts, interpret outputs and maintain human agency while benefiting from AI insights. This is a

cultural, organisational and leadership challenge requiring thoughtful frameworks and illustrative examples.

Complex or merely complicated? Why it matters for decision-making

When organisations face a *complicated* situation, like building a new manufacturing plant or deploying new payroll software, they are dealing with challenges that, whilst difficult, can be broken down into component parts. These situations have clear cause-and-effect relationships that can be analysed and understood, even if doing so requires significant expertise. In complicated situations, past experience is a reliable guide - what worked before will likely work again if properly adapted.

Complex situations are fundamentally different. They involve multiple interconnected elements where cause-and-effect relationships are only apparent in retrospect and cannot be reliably predicted. As Rittel and Webber pointed out in their seminal work[34] on 'wicked problems', complex issues resist complete definition and have no clear stopping points or criteria for success. Examples include transforming organisational culture, entering new markets or evolving service delivery models.

The key differences between complicated and complex situations include:[35]

1. **Predictability:** Complicated situations follow predictable patterns and can be mapped out in advance. Complex situations are inherently emergent - their patterns only become clear as events unfold.

2. **Solutions:** Complicated problems can have 'right' and 'wrong' solutions that can be tested and replicated. Complex challenges have better or worse solutions depending on the circumstances prevailing at a particular point in time. Where a complicated situation might be resolved by an imperative decision (this is what we will do to solve the problem), complex situations may be better tackled by a hypothetical decision (let's try this and see what response we get).

3. **Expertise:** Complicated situations benefit from deep technical expertise in relevant domains. Complex situations require adaptive learning and the integration of multiple perspectives.

4. **Planning:** Complicated projects can be planned in detail with reasonable confidence. Complex initiatives require flexible, iterative approaches that can adapt to emerging conditions.

For decision-making, these differences are crucial. Complicated situations can be addressed through structured analysis, detailed planning and systematic implementation. Complex situations demand a different approach - one that emphasises learning, flexibility and the ability to adapt as understanding develops.

Decision-making for complex situations

To make sure we make decisions in ways that accommodate complexity, we will need a process that:

1. Can consume large amounts of data, insights and decision-options to make the decision-making as richly informed as possible;

2. Breaks the decision-making process down into phases, so we can keep sense-checking our progress, keep incorporating new information and insight and progressively home in on better and better decisions;

3. Ensures our assumptions are challenged, surfaces counter intuitive insights and prompts us to loop back to review and revise the conclusions drawn in previous phases of decision-making;

4. Test potential decisions by running scenario analyses to gain insights into possible decision-outcomes;

5. Encourages decisions that commit to testing and experimentation rather than to predetermined outcomes;

6. Keep humans firmly in the loop throughout decision-making and also enable diverse stakeholder perspectives to be considered to ensure the decision is examined through multiple lenses.

The goal isn't to eliminate uncertainty - which would be impossible given the inherent complexity - but rather to embrace it whilst making the most informed decisions possible.

Key take-aways – why you need to improve your decision-making

The lessons from history, like the fall of Kodak, are clear: in today's fast-paced, data-saturated world, the inability to make good decisions leads to failure more quickly than ever before. This reality demands that we make **faster decisions**, not by being reckless, but by being more agile and responsive to the complex operating environment we now face.

The most critical area for improvement is in high-impact, high-complexity decisions. As we've seen, it is crucial to distinguish between what is merely complicated and what is truly complex. Complicated problems can be solved with expertise and established processes, but complex challenges, with their unpredictable nature and interconnected variables, demand a different approach. To navigate this, we must make **smarter decisions**. This means casting a wider net to explore more possibilities and digging deeper to understand their potential outcomes. It requires a structured approach to harness information without becoming overwhelmed - a challenge where, as we will explore later, AI can be a powerful ally.

Finally, in a world of complexity, there are no perfect, 'correct' answers, only **better decisions** that are more informed, robust and adaptable. By adopting a process specifically designed for the ambiguity of complex situations, we create a consistent, repeatable bias towards these better outcomes, increasing our chances of success where the stakes are highest.

CHAPTER 3: The faster, smarter, better decision-making process

Put 'decision-making process' into a search engine and you will be deluged with a myriad of multi-step process diagrams. The world seems to agree that decisions ought to be made using a five, six or seven step process. Figure 2 shows a selection of how they are visualised.

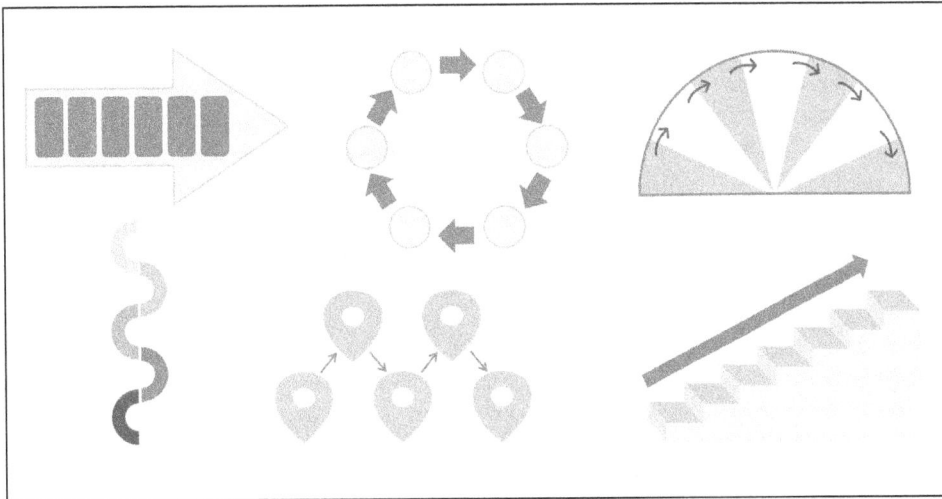

Figure 2 A range of different ways to visualise the decision-making process (adapted from results of a Google Image search for 'decision-making process')

Our search for a process for making faster, smarter, better decisions, therefore, begins with a simple process, as illustrated in Figure 3. It has discrete elements ('phases') progressing from left to right, in a sequential time series. This doesn't, however, mean that all decision-making progresses in that direction. The arrows pointing back in the opposite direction indicate that a key part of decision-making is realising that a previous step in the process needs to be revisited in light of new information having been discovered. This gives us a 'linear-with-loops' process that is common in thinking about complexity. The arrows in the black circles at the junction of adjacent phases in Figure 3 represent the outputs of each phase, which are also the inputs into the next phase.

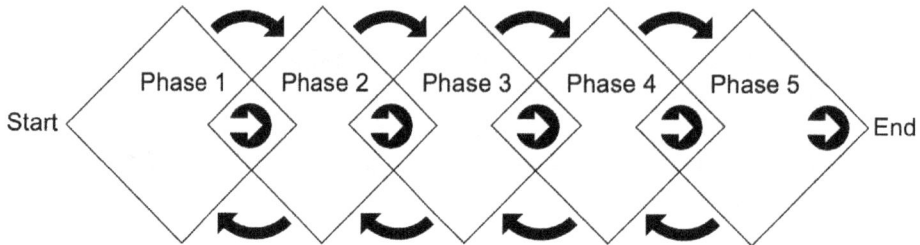

Figure 3 A simple multi-phase process for decision-making

In keeping with this 'linear-with-loops' idea, the elements are called 'phases' rather than 'stages' or steps' to try to indicate the flexibility within the process: a phase is merely a part of a process (e.g. phases of the moon), whereas a stage is typically a defined period of time (e.g. the mountain stage of the Tour de France) and a step is part of a sequence (e.g. the final step in the peace negotiations). Thus, at the end of one phase, the process may continue to the next phase, or it might revert to an earlier phase for the decision to be re-worked.

Let's now go through the phases from the start.

The five phases of the decision-making process

Figure 4 illustrates a model I have evolved over two decades of research and consultancy to be suitable specifically for high-impact, high-complexity decision-making. It originates in my work on both design thinking[36] and on strategy development[37] and, whilst novel in its details, it fits well with the published literature on best-practice decision-making.[38]

Phase 1: Decision Scoping

This foundational phase clearly articulates what decision needs to be made and why it is necessary now. Firstly, through a process of divergent thinking, it explores multiple ways of framing the decision before using convergent thinking to produce a concise written **Decision Brief**. This brief establishes the context, limitations or constraints and the criteria that will be used to assess success.

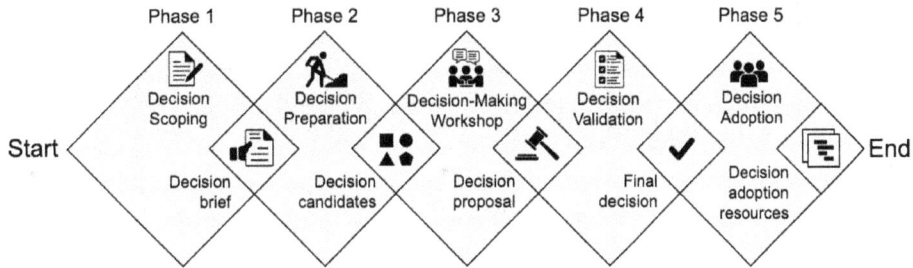

Figure 4 A five-phase decision-making process

Phase 2: Decision Preparation

Decision Preparation builds the knowledge base for making informed choices. This phase begins by exploring a wide range of potential '**decision candidates**' and the '**decision differentiators**' used to compare them. It follows a process of research and analysis to understand the decision landscape – where do all the potential decisions lie, how do they cluster, how do they differ and where will we need to explore to find all the relevant decision-making knowledge associated with them? Some of that information will come from data – product/service data, market data, financial data. Some will come from people – your front-line teams, managers and partner/supplier organisations. Some may come from exploring the web or finding research reports. It is important that this phase of decision-making is well-structured and carefully managed to investigate widely whilst maintaining focus. Done well, **Decision Preparation** adequately informs the decision-makers of both the complexity of the decision they are about to make and the foreseeable implications of the options they have to decide between.. The output of this phase is a **Record of Decision Preparation**, which contains a refined set of contextualised decision candidates and the evidence needed to differentiate them in the next phase.

Phase 3: Decision-Making Workshop

This phase is a robust and formal process designed to bring key decision-makers together and translate the prepared options into a clear choice. The process begins with essential **Pre-Workshop Preparation**, where a briefing document is created to ensure all participants arrive fully informed about the decision candidates, assessment criteria and their own specific roles.

The **Decision-Making Workshop** itself follows a structured, four-activity format. It guides the group from establishing a shared context and exploring all options through to a rigorous analysis and deliberation of the alternatives. By balancing divergent and convergent thinking within this formal structure, the workshop ensures that 'decision candidates' are thoroughly evaluated before the group arrives at a formal **Decision Proposal**.

Phase 4: Decision Validation

This phase rigorously tests the **Decision Proposal** before committing significant resources, strengthening the choice by answering two core questions: "Is it the right decision?" and "Is it a justified decision?". The first question is answered through **Scope Validation**, where the proposal is checked against the original **Decision Brief** to ensure it solves the problem as intended. The second is answered through **Evidence Validation**, a systematic check to ensure the decision's rationale is fully supported by the research and analysis from the **Decision Preparation** phase.

This process deliberately challenges assumptions and surfaces 'blind spots'. It culminates in preparing a formal **Case for the Decision** to secure leadership approval, ensuring the final output is a single, robust and formally validated **Final Decision**.

Phase 5: Decision Adoption

The last phase focuses on turning the validated **Final Decision** into organisational reality through **Decision Adoption**. This phase is deliberately named 'Adoption,' not 'Implementation', to shift the focus from a top-down, mechanical execution of a plan to a more human-centric process. Success depends on how people engage with, commit to and actively adapt their own work in response to the decision.

This people-first approach starts by building, and prioritising, a checklist of 'adoptions activities' that need to be done for the decision to be successfully adopted. Next, the key people involved need to be mapped onto the checklist: who will drive decision adoption, who will play an enabling role and who will be significantly affected? Then an agile Governance Framework is established to define how progress will be tracked, how challenges will be addressed and how change will be accommodated. The Checklist of Adoption Activities and the Governance Framework form part of the final output: a comprehensive pack of Decision Adoption Resources, a living set of documents that will guide the organisation in realising the full value of its decision.

Incorporating 'design thinking' into decision-making

The final refinement of our decision-making process is to build in some design thinking to strengthen our process's ability to deal with complexity. In both The Strategy Manual[39] and the recent book I co-authored with my father, Seaton Baxter, called Deep Design Thinking, I argue[40] that design thinking has certain key characteristics, including repeated cycles of divergent and convergent thinking (Fig. 5).

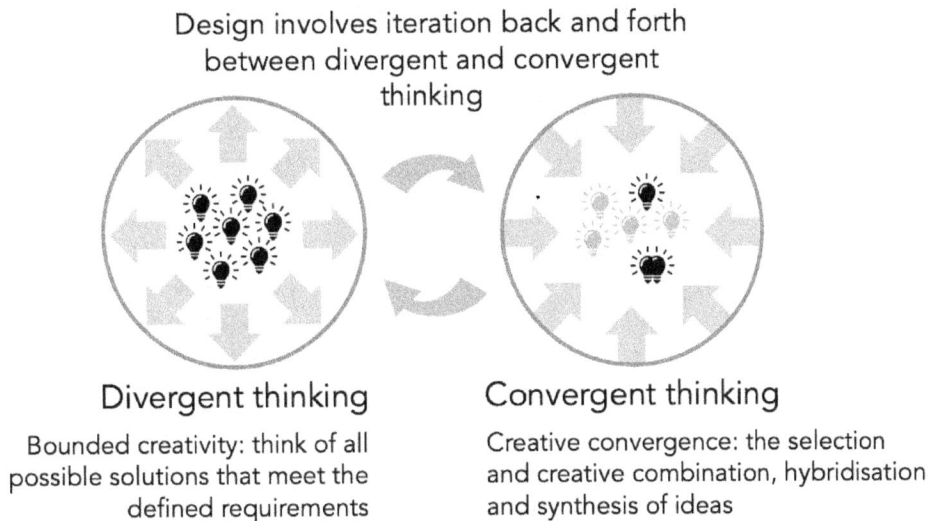

Design involves iteration back and forth between divergent and convergent thinking

Divergent thinking

Bounded creativity: think of all possible solutions that meet the defined requirements

Convergent thinking

Creative convergence: the selection and creative combination, hybridisation and synthesis of ideas

Figure 5 Divergent and convergent thinking (from The Strategy Manual, Baxter, 2020)

The advantage of this type of thinking is that it acknowledges complexity's inherent uncertainty and interconnectedness by first exploring a broad range of possibilities and perspectives before systematically narrowing to actionable solutions. For the first three phases of the decision-making process in particular, such design thinking seems essential, reducing the risk of "if-only-we'd-thought-of-that" errors that often plague rushed decision processes.

Rhythmic alternation between divergent and convergent thinking ensures that decisions benefit from both creative exploration and disciplined focus, ultimately leading to faster, smarter, better outcomes that are both innovative and practical.

Key take-aways – The faster, smarter, better decision-making process

The faster, smarter, better decision-making process introduced in this chapter has the following attributes:

- **A structured five-phase process:** A clear, five-phase process is proposed as the foundation for navigating high-impact, high-complexity decisions. The phases are Decision Scoping, Decision Preparation, Decision-Making Workshop, Decision Validation and Decision Adoption.

- **A flexible and iterative process:** The process is not a rigid, linear path but a 'linear-with-loops' process that allows teams to revisit earlier phases as new information emerges. The use of the term 'phases' rather than 'steps' or 'stages' is deliberate to emphasise this flexibility.

- **The power of design thinking:** The process is strengthened by incorporating repeated cycles of divergent thinking (to explore a wide range of possibilities) and convergent thinking (to narrow focus and synthesise ideas into actionable solutions). This approach ensures decisions are both creative and practical.

- **Clear outputs for each phase:** The process is structured so that each phase produces a distinct output that serves as a key input for the next. For example, the **Decision Brief** from the Decision Scoping phase informs the Decision Preparation phase, and the **Decision Proposal** from the Decision-Making Workshop is tested in the Decision Validation phase, creating a clear and traceable journey.

CHAPTER 4: AI-augmented decisions

This chapter aims to persuade you of the value of AI-augmenting the faster, smarter, better decision-making process presented in Chapter 3 and then to give you a simple, non-technical, step-by-step guide for doing so.

It is the central premise of this book that AI is now capable of usefully and valuably augmenting human decision-making for high-impact, high-complexity decisions. The important disclaimer, however, is that this book is all about using AI to enable humans to make faster, smarter, better decisions, not to make the decisions on our behalf. **Decision-making is always the responsibility of humans. AIs make assumptions and mistakes – always double check their responses.**

Why now is the time for AI-augmented decisions

Artificial intelligence has been supporting human decision-making for decades; much longer than the recent flurry of excitement about Generative AI[41] might suggest. The AI expert systems of the 1990s offered rules-based decision support by codifying expert knowledge in narrow domains.[42] They, however, proved brittle and inflexible, requiring extensive re-programming for each new application. A commonly cited example[43] is the medical expert system that diagnosed a car with patches of rust as having measles. Despite this, expert systems consistently applied analytical frameworks without the fatigue or bias that affects human analysis, making them valuable complements to human judgment in specific data-intensive domains.

Today's AI systems represent a fundamental shift - they can process unstructured information at scale, learn from examples rather than explicit rules and adapt to new contexts. This flexibility, combined with dramatically improved availability (to anyone with a browser), creates new opportunities for augmenting human decision-making across a much broader range of organisational challenges. AI platforms have crossed a key threshold in their linguistic abilities: they are able to take a generic set of instructions and apply them meaningfully and insightfully to a specific situation.

A glossary of AI

Before we begin our journey to AI-augmented decisions, we need a shared understanding of the terminology we are going to use:

Artificial intelligence (AI): the capability of computational systems to perform tasks typically associated with human intelligence, such as learning, reasoning, problem-solving, perception and decision-making.[44]

AI Platform: for practical purposes, most people think of an AI platform as the app or website that enables a user to interact with a specific AI model such as ChatGPT, Claude or Gemini. More technically, an AI platform is an integrated suite of technologies enabling a particular family of foundation models (such as GPT-5, Claude Sonnet 4 or Gemini 2.5) to be accessed and used. [45]

Context window: the amount of information a generative AI model can recall during a session, measured in 'tokens' - the smallest building blocks a model can process, such as a part of a word, image or video. The longer the context window, the more data a model can process and use.[46]

Conversation thread: a single, continuous dialogue between you and the AI. When you start a new chat or conversation with your AI platform, you're creating a fresh thread. Each thread maintains its own context and history.

Generative AI (Gen AI): a subset of artificial intelligence that uses generative models to produce new content, such as text, images or other data. For example, it can be used to draft a marketing email, create a logo concept for a new product or summarise a long report. These models learn the underlying patterns and structures of their training data and use them to generate novel output based on a user's prompt.[47] This is different from Predictive AI, which uses data to extrapolate future trends. For instance, while Predictive AI might produce sales projections based on current marketing plans, Generative AI could suggest new marketing copy by analysing the best- and worst-performing past campaigns.[48]

Large language models (LLMs): best thought of as the 'brain' behind the AI platform you use. An LLM is a specific type of AI that has been trained on a massive amount of text and data, allowing it to understand and generate human-like language. For example, OpenAI's popular ChatGPT service is powered by its family of GPT models (like GPT-5). Increasingly, the term is expanding as the latest models are now **multimodal**, meaning they can understand and process not just text, but also images, charts and even audio. Because they learn from vast internet-scale data, LLMs are incredibly versatile but can also reflect the inaccuracies and biases present in their training material, which is why human oversight is always critical.[49]

Machine learning: The statistical algorithms in an AI platform that enable it to learn from data and generalise to unseen data, thus performing tasks without explicit instructions.[50]

Prompt: In the context of AI, a prompt is the input you provide to a LLM to elicit a specific response. This can take various forms ranging from simple questions or keywords to complex instructions, code snippets or even creative writing samples. The effectiveness of your prompt directly influences the quality and relevance of the AI's output.[51]

Super-prompt: a super-prompt is "an advanced, highly structured prompt that provides an AI system with detailed instructions [and] context [...] that guide the AI to produce the desired output while adhering to specific requirements."[52] For the purposes of this book, a super-prompt is a lengthy, detailed prompt, typically a few thousand words in length, that provides context, instructions or both to enable an AI to guide the person prompting through a highly structured process that forms part of decision-making.

System prompt: An initial, hidden instruction provided to a large language model that establishes its role, tone, behavioural rules and decision-making framework for all subsequent interactions with the user. It typically includes detailed guidelines, examples and constraints that persist throughout a session, shaping how the model interprets and responds to user inputs.[53]

Token: a unit of data that is the smallest building block a generative AI model can process, such as a part of a word, image or video, enabling prediction, generation and reasoning.[54] The size of context windows is typically measured in tokens.

The emergence of decision-augmenting AI capabilities

Clearly, contemporary AI platforms are undergoing rapid technological advancement and are increasing their capabilities at a rate that is hard to keep up with. There are, however, a number of key breakthrough capabilities that have transformed AI's potential for augmenting human decision-making:[55]

1. Expanded context windows

The dramatic growth in context window size has revolutionised AI's ability to work with comprehensive information. Early AI assistants could only process a few sentences at once, while today's systems can analyse entire documents or conversations spanning hundreds of thousands of words.[56]

This expansion transforms decision support by allowing AI to:

- maintain coherence across lengthy analyses;
- connect insights from different sections of long documents;
- consider multiple information sources simultaneously.

Decision-makers can now work with AI on complex scenarios without artificial constraints on information scope.

2. Multimodal processing

Contemporary AI systems have transcended text-only processing to work across different information types. Several AI systems can now analyse images, charts and diagrams alongside text, extracting insights from visual data that earlier systems couldn't access.[57]

This capability significantly enhances decision support in domains where critical information spans multiple formats. A healthcare decision might involve medical imaging and patient records; a financial decision might require analysis of market visualisations alongside written reports; an operational decision might depend on process diagrams with accompanying performance metrics.

3. Retrieval-Augmented Generation (RAG)

The integration of external knowledge retrieval with generative capabilities has addressed a critical limitation of earlier AI systems. By pulling relevant information from external sources at runtime, modern AI can incorporate up-to-date, accurate information rather than relying solely on knowledge encoded in its parameters.[58]

For decision-makers, this means AI analyses can include the latest market data, recent research findings or organisation-specific information, dramatically enhancing their relevance and reliability for time-sensitive decisions.

These capabilities collectively transform AI from a narrowly focused analytical tool to a versatile thinking partner that can engage with the full complexity of high-impact, high-complexity decisions. The remainder of this chapter explores how these capabilities can be applied effectively within our five-phase decision-making process to create faster, smarter, better organisational decisions.

4. Chain of thought reasoning

Modern AI systems can now work through problems step-by-step, making their thinking process transparent rather than delivering black-box answers. When Google researchers introduced chain-of-thought prompting in 2022,[59] they demonstrated that this approach made large language models significantly more accurate at complex reasoning tasks like mathematical problem-solving and logical deduction.

For decision-makers, this transparency is transformative. Rather than receiving unexplained recommendations, they can now see the logical path the AI followed, enabling them to evaluate assumptions, spot potential flaws and build deeper understanding of the problem space.

The benefits of AI-augmented decisions

Working together, human intelligence and AI augmentation make a remarkable partnership. Human intelligence brings two distinct and powerful advantages to the decision-making process. The first is a sophisticated understanding of the organisation's human elements: its social contexts, power dynamics and complex stakeholder networks. The second is a deep, often intuitive, grasp of the complex operational systems and processes that underpin how the organisation functions. This systemic understanding, built through years of direct experience, allows human decision-makers to appreciate not just the formal workflows, but the unwritten rules, hidden dependencies and practical realities that govern how value is created and delivered.

Human intelligence brings a deep understanding of context, but it also has inherent limits. The first is a staggering disparity in information processing speed compared to artificial intelligence. As shown in Figure 6,[60] AI hardware is millions of times faster than its biological equivalents. While this comparison is a simplification, the practical implication is profound: a task that would take a human a year could be processed by an AI in seconds. The second limitation is our susceptibility to cognitive biases that distort our judgment. We instinctively seek evidence that confirms our beliefs while dismissing contradictory information, and we are often blind to patterns that lie outside our personal experience. It is this combination of limited speed and unconscious bias that makes the case for AI-augmented decision-making so compelling.

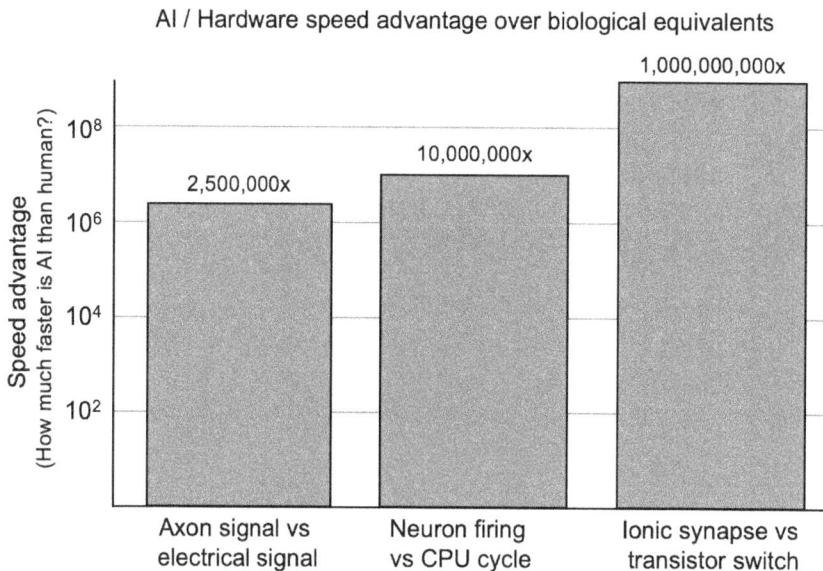

AI / Hardware speed advantage over biological equivalents

Figure 6 *Speed advantage that AI has over humans in information processing*

AI systems also excel at identifying patterns across large datasets that transcend the experience of any individual human, surfacing counterintuitive connections and challenging assumptions that might otherwise go unexamined. They can analyse historical decisions and outcomes across many organisations, detecting subtle patterns of success and failure that might escape human notice.

This complementarity creates a powerful synthesis: we can leverage our own deep understanding of organisational dynamics and stakeholder needs while using AI insights to expand our consideration set, pressure-test our assumptions and keep our cognitive biases in check. Combining human and artificial intelligence creates a decision-making approach that is both more comprehensive and more balanced than either could achieve independently.

AI-augmented decision-making, therefore, is built on core principles of methodical exploration, diverse perspectives and iterative refinement. This approach recognises limits on both human thinking and AI-based analysis and seeks to leverage the complementary strengths of both.

Specifically, let's explore how AI can help us make faster decisions, smarter decisions and better decisions:

Faster decisions

- **Information retrieval and synthesis:** AI can process vast amounts of unstructured data in seconds, condensing hours of research into moments.

- **Scenario generation:** AI can rapidly create multiple decision scenarios and preliminary analyses that would take teams days to develop.

- **Process acceleration:** AI can streamline administrative aspects of decision processes (documentation, meeting summaries, action tracking etc.) that typically slow progress.

- **Real-time insights:** During decision discussions, AI can provide immediate answers to questions that arise, eliminating delays waiting for information.

Smarter decisions

- **Pattern recognition across siloed data:** AI can identify connections between seemingly unrelated information sources that humans might miss.

- **Cognitive bias mitigation:** AI can systematically flag potential biases in reasoning and offer alternative perspectives.

- **Expertise amplification:** AI allows decision-makers to quickly tap into knowledge domains outside their expertise without lengthy consultation processes.

- **Counterfactual thinking:** AI excels at generating "what if" scenarios that challenge conventional thinking and reveal overlooked possibilities.

Better decisions (especially for complex situations)

- **Nuanced evaluation:** AI can help assess options against multiple criteria simultaneously, with explicit weighting of different factors.

- **Adaptive reasoning:** Instead of seeking single 'right' answers, AI can help organisations understand decision trade-offs and design options that evolve with changing circumstances.

- **Stakeholder impact modelling:** AI can simulate how decisions might affect different stakeholders, helping organisations design more balanced approaches.

- **Adoption pathway mapping:** AI can help identify potential obstacles and enablers for executing decisions, improving follow-through.

In essence, the synergy between human and artificial intelligence creates a decision-making capability greater than the sum of its parts. This partnership allows us to make **faster** decisions by rapidly processing information and accelerating workflows, **smarter** decisions by uncovering hidden patterns and challenging our inherent biases and, ultimately, **better** decisions by enabling a more nuanced and adaptive approach to complexity. It is this powerful combination that provides a robust response to the challenges of modern decision-making.

These benefits, however, are not automatic. They depend on a structured approach that effectively channels AI's power. Having established why this partnership is so valuable, the following section will turn to the practicalities of how to set up and use AI platforms to bring these augmented decisions to life.

Getting started using AI platforms

Getting a feel for the practicalities of AI-augmentation couldn't be much easier. Start by just jumping on an AI platform – at the time of writing, the most popular platforms are:

- ChatGPT[61]
- Google's Gemini[62]
- Anthropic's Claude[63]
- xAI's Grok[64]
- DeepSeek[65]

It is usually best to log in. Some platforms require you to, and most offer enhanced functionality once you are logged in.

If you haven't used AI much, try asking different types of questions to get a feel for how it responds. Here are some simple prompts:

- *"My favourite food is Italian. Can you suggest some unusual twists on favourite recipes"*

- *"When it is raining, will I stay drier by running or walking and can you explain why?"*

- *"I'm an action / sci-fi movie fan and my flat-mate is more into rom-coms – any suggestions on movies that we'd both like?"*

- *"Has there been an increase in the number of wars being fought compared to 50 years ago?"*

Ask follow-up questions to engage the AI in more of a conversation. If you ever find yourself struggling, just ask the AI for advice: *"What would be a good follow-up question?"*

From Prompts to Context Engineering

Advice abounds on how to design the perfect prompt – just try searching for 'how to write AI prompts' and you'll have plenty to choose from. Andrej Karpathy, formerly an AI leader/founder at both OpenAI and Tesla, however, suggests[66] that 'context engineering' is a better way to think about working with prompts. Context engineering moves beyond simple prompt design to systematically optimising information payloads for LLMs. This marks a shift from the 'art' of prompt design to the 'science' of information logistics and system optimisation. Mei et al[67] reconceptualise the context we provide to an AI not as a single, static string of text but as a "dynamically structured set of informational components". These components can include:

- **System instructions and rules:** The core directives for the AI's behaviour;

- **External knowledge:** Information retrieved from outside sources to ground the AI's responses;

- **Persistent memory:** Information from previous interactions to maintain coherence;

- **The user's immediate request:** The specific question or task at hand.

This move from simple prompting to context engineering is more than a preference; it's a reflection of how AI models technically operate. Whenever we start a new chat with an AI, that AI pre-loads a 'system prompt', telling the AI how to interact. The system prompt for Anthropic's Claude, [68] for example, is thought to be almost 10,000 words long and contains instructions such as:

- "when in casual conversations, use sentences and paragraphs rather than bullet lists";

- "maintain a conversational tone even in cases where Claude is unable or unwilling to help the person with all or part of their task";

- "when asked product questions related to Claude or Anthropic, Claude should tell them it doesn't know, and point them to 'https://support.anthropic.com'";

- "Claude answers from its own extensive knowledge first for stable information. For time-sensitive topics or when users explicitly need current information, search immediately".

Context engineering sets out to provide complete and structured information to an AI about the intention of the conversation and the constraints and guidelines to be followed in pursuit of that intention. It is all about giving the AI a rich and nuanced way to frame your request rather than trying to find clever ways to articulate that request. This is the premise of the 'super-prompts' used in this book which provide both context and instructions to enable your AI to guide you through the decision-making process. Whilst the super-prompts we will be using are several pages long (you can find them in the Appendices), the example below illustrates how you can bring rich context into your own AI prompts:

> *"I am a businesswoman with a long career in marketing and sales for a variety of large and small organisations and am looking for advice and guidance to help me write my first novel. I have written extensively for my work, including copy for marketing and advertising campaigns and scripts for consultative sales negotiations. I have also written articles and presentations for the trade press. I am aware that many universities offer courses on creative writing and that many published books promise the secrets of success in writing fiction. What I'd like you to help me find out is the top tips for new fiction writers that are most consistently offered, most highly regarded and most practical for me to apply to my emerging writing practice. These top tips could be about writing habits (e.g. get up early and write every day), the writing process (e.g. produce the first draft quickly and with few revisions) or writing outcomes (e.g. many stories follow a hero's journey)."*

By including personal context, a high-level intention and a specific 'ask', this example provides sufficient context to prompt an in-depth, highly specific response – to get a feel for context engineering, try entering a prompt like this into your own AI.

Okay, enough initial experimentation. Time to move on to some serious AI-augmented decisions.

Deciding on your AI Platform

In order to get acquainted with the workings of AI, it really doesn't matter which AI platform you choose. However, for professional work within an organisation, it can matter a lot. The key issue is data security. If, for example, you get Gemini to help you make some critical decisions for your organisation, have you just shared your most precious secrets with Google in the process? The answer, at the time of writing, is yes, if you access Gemini via its web address and don't change your default settings. Google Gemini's privacy hub[69] explains that, by default, Google will store all your Gemini chats and everything you upload to Gemini in the course of these chats for human reviewers to access for quality control and product improvement purposes.

Most AI platforms offer enterprise cloud access[70] that safeguards all private data, but **before giving any AI platform access to any sensitive information from your organisation, make sure you are acting in compliance with your own organisation's AI policies and standards.** If you don't have any such policies and standards, guidance on data and security issues can be found from the National Cyber-Security Centre in the USA[71] or from the Information Commissioner's Office in the UK.[72]

If these policies and standards prevent you using the openly accessible AI platforms, such as ChatGPT, Gemini or Claude, you may be able to run an open-source AI platform on a local machine. For a simple guide on how to try this out, see The Neuron's explainer.[73]

Assuming you are now able to navigate your way around your own organisation's data security rules, there is one final, and quite tricky, issue to check before finalising your choice of AI platform. This is the platform's 'context window' but before we can do this we need to understand how the process of AI-augmented decisions actually works and how it determines the size of context window required. So, we will return to this at the end of this chapter.

As for my own choice of AI, my work for this book was undertaken partly on Claude Sonnet[74] (first 3.5 and then 3.7) under their Pro Plan (£170/year, when paid annually) and then on Google Gemini 2.5 Pro. When I needed to undertake deep research into online sources online, I started using Deep Research[75] within Perplexity[76] (£150/year, when paid annually), although more recently (April 2025) I used versions of ChatGPT-4o[77] and Google Gemini 2.5 Pro[78] more for this. I also use Google's NotebookLM[79] as a 'walled garden' where I can upload a bunch of files from my own server and/or point to web pages, YouTube videos etc and undertake analysis of just those sources.

Super-prompts: the key to AI-augmented decisions

For the purposes of this book, a **super-prompt** is a lengthy, detailed prompt that functions in the same way as an AI's own **system prompt**. Typically a few thousand words long, it provides the AI with the specific context, instructions, rules, and expert knowledge required to guide a user through a highly structured process, such as a phase of decision-making. This provides the AI with a rich, multi-faceted understanding of the task, enabling it to act as a more effective partner in the structured decision-making process.

In the last chapter we explored the five phases of the decision-making process. The AI-augmentation of this process comes from a series of super-prompts, one for each phase of the process. According to our Glossary above, a super-prompt is "an advanced, highly structured prompt that provides an AI system with detailed instructions [and] context [...] that guide the AI to produce the desired output while adhering to specific requirements." [80]

While system prompts are typically hidden, our super-prompts make the domain of good decision-making legible and actionable by the AI in a completely open way. You are not just asking a question; you are configuring the AI to act as an expert partner in a well-defined process, much like an engineer uses a configuration file to define a piece of software's core behaviour.

So, for example, the super-prompt for Decision Scoping is a series of instructions that enables the AI to walk the person prompting through the scoping process and guide them to define the decision, scope out the work needed to make the decision and set out acceptance criteria for the decision, once made. The super-prompts for each phase of decision-making can be read in the Appendices and downloaded from the Goal Atlas web site (goalatlas.com/ai-augmented-decisions) via the QR code below. All the super-prompts in this book are shared under Creative Commons license (CC BY 4.0)[81] so they can be freely used and adapted (with attribution to Goal Atlas Ltd).

The super-prompts in this book are designed to encapsulate domain expertise about good decision-making, whilst giving the AI a leadership role in guiding their human prompter through a good-practice process for decision-making. They have been derived from research in psychology, business management and complexity theory and also from my 20+ years of consultancy practice, facilitating decision-making by leaders of both businesses and third sector organisations. These generic, reusable super-prompts can be used for any complex decision.

Using prompts and super-prompts

AI platforms typically have an 'add', '+' or 'upload' feature allowing you to input text, code, images, PDFs etc. The entire AI-augmented decisions process begins by uploading the first super-prompt on **Decision Scoping** (see Appendix 1a) into your chosen AI platform (Fig. 7).

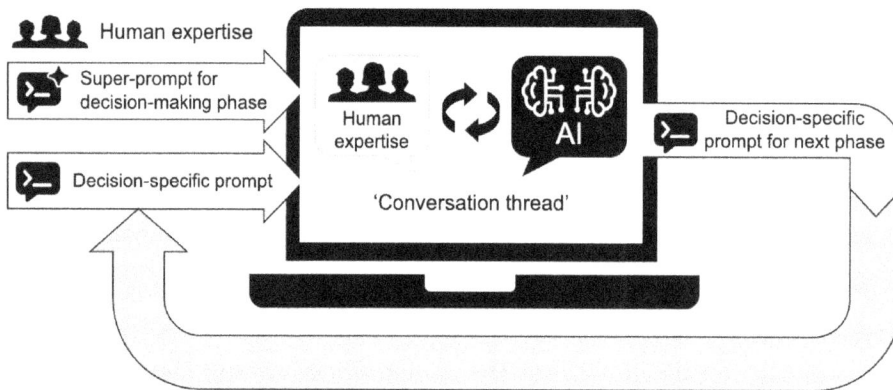

Figure 7 Using prompts and super-prompts

You now need to tell the AI what decision you want to work on by giving it an initial 'decision-specific prompt'. The example used for illustration in Chapters 5 to 9 is the complex, but intuitive and non-technical, decision of 'choosing the holiday of a lifetime'. In this case, the decision to be worked on can be described in the prompt with just those six words. By contrast, some decisions within mid- to large-sized organisations are likely to need much more extensive decision-specific prompts. In which case you can upload a file or files that describe or provide:

1. a description of the decision;

2. the organisational context for this decision;

3. any key background documents needed to make sense of this decision.

Once the **Decision Scoping Super-prompt** and any files specifying the 'decision-to-be-worked-on' are uploaded, the conversation thread with the AI can be started with a simple instruction, such as:

I have just uploaded the Decision Scoping Super-prompt. I would like you to work through the process specified in this document. The specific decision I'd like you to apply this process to is <enter your decision here / "specified in the attached file(s)">.

The AI will then guide you through an extensive conversation to produce a **Decision Brief** for the specific decision you are working on. At the end of that conversation, you will be prompted to download or copy-and-save the resulting **Decision Brief** document that you have just produced.

This **Decision Brief** is then used as one of two prompts for the second phase of the decision-making process: **Decision Preparation**. The other prompt is, of course, the **Decision Preparation Super-prompt**. This process then repeats for the other phases of the decision-making process: the outputs of the preceding stages are used as the decision-specific prompts for the succeeding stage, along with the super-prompt for that phase, as shown in Figure 7.

Conversation threads and context windows

Interactions with AIs are typically defined as 'conversation threads'. These are a sequence of prompts from you and responses from the AI within the one chat. If you start a 'new chat', this generally wipes the AI's memory of the previous chat (although some platforms, such as ChatGPT[82] enable you to select a setting to reference previous chats as a way to inform responses in a new chat).

If we imagine running straight through the entire five phases of an AI-augmented decision, that would be a very long conversation thread. So, from a purely practical point of view, it is probably better to separate them into five discrete conversation threads. This would be done by starting a new chat at the beginning of each phase. To enable this to work smoothly, every super-prompt sets out the context for the entire process and locates where the current phase fits into that entire process.

It turns out that this also works well from a process management point of view. Knowing that each phase needs to be fully complete and the outputs downloaded and saved before the conversation thread is closed, forces a pause and a mental check that everything that needs to be thought of in this phase of decision-making has been thought of.

There are also technical reasons for having several shorter conversation threads rather than one long one. AIs have 'context windows' defining how much information they can hold and make sense of. The size of a context window is measured in 'tokens', and a token is representation of the smallest unit of text the AI can understand and process.[83] Tokens can include whole words, parts of words or even a character or punctuation mark, depending on how the text is broken down (i.e. 'tokenised'). So, for example, the word 'unhappiness' would normally be represented by three tokens: 'happi' – a dimension of human experience; 'ness' – the state of having that experience and 'un' – indicating the absence-of or opposite-of.

The super-prompts in this book range from 2,000 words to almost 4,500, with an average of 3,300. The rule of thumb is to estimate 4 tokens for 3 words.[84] This means that to represent an average super-prompt would require just under 4,500 tokens.

Context windows are also used to remember the back-and-forth conversations between the AI and the person prompting them. For the holiday-of-a-lifetime case study used in this book, these conversations amounted, on average, to just under 6,000 words (8,000 tokens) for each phase of decision-making. This should probably be thought of as a lower boundary. High-impact, high-complexity decisions within organisations are likely to require a lot more discussion than choosing the holiday of a lifetime. Even taking this into account, we might be thinking of 15,000 to 20,000 tokens needed for the super-prompts and the ensuing conversation (for a single phase of the decision-making process in this book). How does that compare with the context windows on AI platforms? Fortunately, context windows have gone from 2,000 tokens in ChatGPT3 in 2020 to 1,000,000 tokens in Google Gemini 2.5 Pro in 2025, a 500-fold increase. Table 1 shows the context windows for some of the leading AI platforms at the time of writing.[85]

Now, whilst it might appear that the ~20,000 tokens needed for a super-prompt and the ensuing conversation doesn't make much of a dent in the 200,000 token capacity of Claude, this misses one crucial factor. How much information are you going to want to upload in order to inform and guide the decision? If, by any chance, you happened to work for a FTSE 100 Company and wanted to upload your latest annual report, they, on average, amount to 153,000 words[86] and hence would need a 200,000 token

Table 1 *Context windows for leading AI Platforms*

AI Platform	Context window (tokens)	Equivalent words
Anthropic's Claude	200,000	150,000
Open AI's Chat GPT	400,000	300,000
Google's Gemini	1,000,000	750,000

window for this on its own. Under these circumstances you have already exceeded the context window capacity of all but Google Gemini.

An entire annual report from a FTSE 100 company, however, is unlikely to be necessary for any decision, even in the company whose report it is. The point is that, even though these context windows look enormous, you cannot just keep on stuffing huge reports into them and expect the AI to keep track of them all.

So, keep each phase of AI-augmented decision-making in its own conversation thread and start a new chat whenever you move on to the next phase. This keeps the context windows required to a reasonable size and maintains a tight contextual focus for the AI.

Key take-aways – AI-augmented decisions

This chapter has established that now is the time to embrace AI-augmented decision-making, moving beyond the hype to practical application. Here are the key take-aways:

- **A new era of decision support:** Today's AI platforms represent a fundamental leap from older expert systems. Breakthroughs like massive context windows, multimodal processing and chain-of-thought reasoning have transformed AI from a rigid analytical tool into a versatile thinking partner. These advancements allow AI to handle unstructured information at scale and apply generic instructions to specific, complex problems, a capability that was previously out of reach.

- **The power of human-AI collaboration:** The most effective decision-making combines the strengths of human intelligence with the capabilities of AI. Humans provide an essential understanding of organisational context, culture and stakeholder dynamics while AI offers incredible speed, the ability to identify patterns across vast datasets and a vital check against our inherent cognitive biases.

- **Delivering faster, smarter, better decisions:** AI augmentation directly addresses the core challenges of modern decision-making. It helps us make:

  a. **Faster decisions** by rapidly retrieving and synthesising information, accelerating the entire process.

  b. **Smarter decisions** by uncovering hidden connections in data, mitigating cognitive biases and amplifying expert knowledge.

  c. **Better decisions** by enabling more nuanced evaluation of complex options and simulating potential outcomes and stakeholder impacts.

- **A structured approach is essential:** Realising these benefits is not automatic; it requires a structured and deliberate methodology. Using 'super-prompts' to guide the AI through a proven, multi-phase process provides the necessary framework. This approach ensures that AI's power is channelled effectively, making the domain of good decision-making legible and actionable for the AI.

- **Practical steps to get started:** Getting started is straightforward but requires attention to practical details. While experimenting with public AI platforms is easy, professional use demands careful consideration of data security and the technical capabilities of your chosen platform, particularly its context window size. Starting with discrete conversation threads for each phase of the decision process is a practical way to manage complexity and stay within technical limits.

Having explored the background to AI-augmented decisions, the next five chapters operate as a practical guide to take you, and your chosen AI, through each of the five decision-making phases in turn:

- Chapter 5: Decision Scoping

- Chapter 6: Decision Preparation

- Chapter 7: Decision-Making Workshop

- Chapter 8: Decision Validation

- Chapter 9: Decision Adoption

CHAPTER 5: Decision Scoping

Introduction & overview

This chapter explains how to scope the decision you need to make and produce a **Decision Brief** - the foundational document in the AI-augmented decision-making process. **Decision Scoping** is the first phase of a five-phase process for AI-augmented decisions, as shown previously in Figure 4.

What is Decision Scoping?

When we scope an activity, we outline its key requirements, objectives and context. The output from scoping is often a 'brief', which will guide and constrain the activity moving forwards.

Creative, design and engineering projects, for example, typically have a brief. This type of brief begins with a project overview/background that provides context, business goals and project rationale. Then it will define the objectives/goals sought: what are the desired outcomes, deliverables and success metrics? A timeline will set out future milestones, deadlines and project phases. Finally, the brief will set out requirements (functional specifications, deliverables, quality standards) and constraints (budget, technical limitations, resource availability, brand guidelines).

By contrast, a **legal brief**, whilst similarly structured, has key differences in its content:

- The project overview/background is less about goals and more about statements of fact and case background. It is focused on past events relevant to legal issues;

- The objectives/goals define the specific legal remedies or court actions sought, focusing on legal outcomes;

- The timeline will specify filing deadlines and procedural dates, rather than project planning;

- The constraints will be about jurisdictional limits, procedural rules and precedent constraints, whilst the requirements will set out court-mandated formatting, citation rules and submission requirements that must be followed.

The Decision Brief

Decision Scoping aims to produce a **Decision Brief** that combines forward-looking aspects of a creative brief with the rigor of a legal brief. It consists of the following core activities:

1. Defining the decision to be made;
2. Identifying work to be done to be able to make the decision;
3. Specifying acceptance criteria for evaluating success so that the ultimate decision made meets our needs.

These activities initially produce a 'draft' **Decision Brief** that can then be focused and refined to produce a 'final' **Decision Brief**, a document that forms the basis of all further decision-making. The brief acts as both a guide to focus our thinking and a reference point to ensure we do not lose sight of where we are trying to get to.

The 'final' **Decision Brief** we end up with indicates an intention that it will remain unchanged. This, however, is an intention rather than an unbreakable rule.

If the **Decision Brief** is to provide criteria for evaluating success and establish boundaries to keep decision-making focused, it is tempting to think it shouldn't change. It should remain a reference document that can be continually checked to make sure your work is still on-track and hasn't suffered scope-creep. This, however, will sometimes prove overly restrictive. Exploring any complex situation will progressively reveal new issues to be considered, new challenges to be overcome and new objectives to aim for. The secret, therefore, is to make changes in a considered and deliberate way. Changes need to be tracked and justified. Change-approval may need to be part of the management of the whole decision-making process.

This flexibility reflects a core principle of the entire five-phase process, which allows for iteration and revisiting earlier steps when significant new insights emerge. A key part of changing the **Decision Brief**, therefore, is to ensure the changes are a genuine reflection of a change in your understanding of the scope of the decision. The brief must never be changed simply to move a decision from out-of-scope to in-scope.

Decision Scoping – the process

We saw in Chapter 3 that incorporating design thinking into complex decision-making can help mitigate the effects of uncertainty and interconnectedness. By repeating cycles of convergent and divergent thinking we explore a broad range of possibilities and perspectives before systematically narrowing to actionable solutions.

In the divergent thinking stage of **Decision Scoping,** we open our minds to multiple ways of defining the decision itself, considering various angles and perspectives that might reshape our understanding of what needs to be decided. We simultaneously explore a comprehensive range of preparatory work that might inform the decision, casting a wide net to ensure no important avenue of investigation is overlooked. This exploration extends to developing diverse acceptance criteria that could potentially evaluate the final decision's quality and challenging fundamental assumptions about the decision's scope, importance, and context. The output of this divergent phase is a draft **Decision Brief**.

After this broad exploration, convergent thinking narrows our focus to craft a precise, well-defined statement of the decision that clearly articulates what needs to be decided. We prioritise a focused set of preparatory work tasks, selecting only those essential for truly informed decision-making. Our acceptance criteria undergo similar refinement, distilling them to those that will best measure decision success. The outcome is a cohesive final **Decision Brief** that provides clear direction while ensuring the decision has been considered from multiple perspectives.

Decision Scoping to produce a **Decision Brief** consists of the five activities described below:

Activity #1 - Defining the decision

What is the decision? This defines the decision that needs to be made and explains why that decision is needed now. Poorly defined decisions can lead to wasted time and effort, which in turn can lead to mis-aligned actions and sub-optimal outcomes. So, by the time the **Decision Brief** is signed off, you need to have nailed the definition of the decision you are setting out to make. This requires your first thoughts about the decision to be presented, but then elaborated, challenged and refined. It may well be that those first thoughts about the decision were right all along, but working through alternatives gives you the confidence that the decision has been well defined.

Activity #2 - Identifying work to be done

What work is needed to prepare for and make the decision? What analysis and insights will be needed to inform the decision? This ought to cover:

a. Analysis of the challenge necessitating the decision. What is the opportunity to be seized or the problem to be resolved? How can the challenge be quantified? Are there any contingencies – will it only be a challenge under certain circumstances?

b. Analysis of the context surrounding the decision. Who will do all the decision preparation and how will they approach that work? Who will be involved in the decision-making and in what roles? Which people and processes will be affected by the decision, once it is made and adopted? Are there any critical dependencies or time pressures?

c. Analysis of the benefits expected to accrue from making the decision. What good will come of it? What harm will be avoided? What factors, if any, will influence the magnitude of its impact? What would happen if no decision were made?

d. An outline timetable for the decision-making process and an indication of the type of people who will need to be involved.

This work only needs to be scoped. It is all too easy here to slip from the **Decision Brief**, where we are merely setting out what needs to be done, to **Decision Preparation** where we actually do the work and find the answers needed to inform the decision making. So, stay disciplined and stick to proposing what work will need to be done.

Activity #3 - Specifying acceptance criteria

What criteria could be used to assess whether any decisions made are good enough? These could be minimum acceptance criteria and/or excellence criteria. Deciding these up-front is an essential part of quality-controlling the decision-making process. It is also an excellent defence against several cognitive biases on the part of the decision-makers. For example, under time pressure, decision-makers will often opt for the first option that seems good enough. This, however, may turn out to be a compelling story that doesn't stand up to scrutiny against objective evidence. Philosophers have a name for this type of decision – it is called 'defeasible reasoning'[87] – and, as the name suggests, it is an error of reasoning. Since such errors are so important for decision-makers to avoid, this is why we need to take the time to produce acceptance criteria as part of the **Decision Brief**.

Activity #4 - Producing a draft Decision Brief

Activities #1 to #3 can be compiled into a first draft of the **Decision Brief** that contains a definition of the decision, an overview of the work to be done to prepare for and make the decision and a record of the acceptance criteria to evaluate whether the decision you eventually make is a good decision.

Activity #5 - Producing a final Decision Brief

The final step uses creative convergence to 'tighten' or 'narrow' the draft **Decision Brief** to ensure the clarity and effectiveness of the decision definition, the work to be done and the acceptance criteria within the final version of the brief.

This rigorous approach to **Decision Scoping** ensures a well-crafted **Decision Brief** that serves two key purposes:

1. It informs, shapes and supports subsequent phases of decision-making:

    - It guides **Decision Preparation** (Chapter 6) by defining required analysis and information gathering;

    - It provides the framework for the **Decision-Making Workshop** (Chapter 7) by making the decision well-informed and purposeful;

    - It enables effective **Decision Validation** (Chapter 8) by providing key acceptance criteria against which the decision will be judged;

    - It supports robust **Decision Adoption** (Chapter 9) by creating a clear record of intent.

2. It makes the overall decision-making process more robust in several important ways:

    - It aligns stakeholders on what needs to be decided and why;

    - It surfaces hidden assumptions before they cause problems;

    - It creates clear criteria for evaluating success;

    - It establishes boundaries that keep the process focused.

AI-augmenting the Decision Scoping process

Artificial intelligence transforms **Decision Scoping** from what might be a linear, potentially narrow exercise into a structured, comprehensive process that thoroughly explores the decision space before focusing. Rather than simply helping to document a predetermined decision definition, AI serves as a thinking partner that systematically guides users through divergent and convergent thinking phases. For instance, during divergent thinking, the AI might prompt you to consider the decision from overlooked stakeholder perspectives, suggest alternative ways to frame the challenge based on different contexts, or explore extreme variations of potential solutions, techniques designed to push beyond initial assumptions.

Enhancing divergent thinking

AI excels at expanding the exploration of decision definitions in several key ways:

- **Multiple perspective generation:** AI can systematically explore diverse ways to frame the decision, helping identify nuances and dimensions that might be overlooked in traditional approaches.

- **Assumption identification:** AI can surface implicit assumptions embedded in initial decision definitions, enabling more thorough examination of underlying premises.

- **Contextual reframing:** Beyond considering obvious formulations, AI can reframe the decision through different temporal, stakeholder and environmental lenses.

- **Work-to-be-done exploration:** AI helps identify a comprehensive range of preparation activities across different knowledge domains, ensuring thorough consideration of what's needed for quality decision-making.

- **Acceptance criteria development:** AI can generate diverse evaluation frameworks that encompass both quantitative metrics and qualitative factors, creating a more robust foundation for eventual decision assessment.

Supporting convergent thinking

After broad exploration, AI provides sophisticated support for focusing and synthesising:

- **Pattern recognition:** AI can identify connections and relationships between different potential decision definitions, helping distil multiple perspectives into coherent alternatives.

- **Consistency evaluation:** AI excels at checking for alignment between decision definitions, proposed preparation activities and acceptance criteria, ensuring the final brief forms a cohesive whole.

- **Creative synthesis:** Rather than simply selecting from among options, AI can combine elements from different formulations to create hybrid approaches that capture the strengths of multiple perspectives.

- **Logic and coherence checking:** AI systematically evaluates whether the converged **Decision Brief** is internally consistent and comprehensive enough to guide subsequent phases effectively.

The goal of AI augmentation of **Decision Scoping** isn't to automate the process but to make it more thorough and thoughtful. By systematically exploring the decision from multiple angles, AI helps decision-makers establish a clearer, more comprehensive foundation for all subsequent phases while maintaining human judgment at the centre of the process. This human-AI partnership involves the AI acting as an expert guide, asking clarifying questions, frequently checking your understanding, and ensuring a balance between thorough exploration and efficient progress, while also managing the outputs by offering summaries and records at key stages.

Output: Decision Brief

The output from **Decision Scoping** (and hence the input into the **Decision Preparation**) is the **Decision Brief**. This is the foundational document upon which all subsequent phases will be built. The **Decision Brief** contains a succinct definition of the decision to be made, an overview of the work that needs to be done in order to make the decision and the acceptance criteria that will quality control the decision once it is reached. Note that within the **Decision Scoping** phase we will distinguish between draft and final **Decision Brief.** For the rest of the decision-making process, however, we can simply refer to the '**Decision Brief'**, produced as the output from **Decision Scoping**.

Your instructions for starting Decision Scoping

1. Choose your AI platform (see Chapter 4's 'Deciding on your AI Platform' for guidance on this).

2. Download the **Decision Scoping Super-prompt** (given in **Appendix 1a**) from goalatlas.com/ai-augmented-decisions via the QR code below.

Note: Whilst the purpose of this chapter has been to give you an overview of the process of **Decision Scoping**, you are welcome to read the full **Decision Scoping Super-prompt** in Appendix 1a to understand the specific instructions the AI will be given.

3. Upload this super-prompt to your AI platform.

4. Do one of the following (see Chapter 4's 'Using prompts and super-prompts'):

    a. Start the chat by directly typing in your decision-specific prompt to your AI, such as:

    I have just uploaded the Decision Scoping Super-prompt. I would like you to work through the process specified in this document. The specific decision I'd like you to apply this process to is <enter your decision here>.

    b. Upload a file or files describing the decision you want to start scoping and start the chat by typing the following prompt:

    I have just uploaded the Decision Scoping Super-prompt. I would like you to work through the process specified in this document. The specific decision I'd like you to apply this process to is specified in the attached file(s).

The AI will then guide you through an extensive conversation to produce a **Decision Brief** for the specific decision you are working on. At the end of that conversation, you will be prompted to download or copy-and-save the resulting **Decision Brief** document that you have just produced.

An example of AI-augmented Decision Scoping

The example we are going to work on throughout this book is 'choosing the holiday of a lifetime', a readily grasped concept that I hope you can imagine, even if the whole idea of a holiday of a lifetime is not your thing. 'Choosing the holiday of a lifetime', however, is still quite a complex challenge with a number of potential emergent features to keep things interesting whilst illustrating each phase of the AI-augmented decision-making process.

The AI I chose to use throughout this case study was Google Gemini 2.5 Pro.[88] Following the instructions above, I uploaded the **Decision Scoping Super-prompt** and entered this decision-specific prompt:

> *I have just uploaded the Decision Scoping Super-prompt. I would like you to work through the process specified in this document. The specific decision I'd like you to apply this process to is 'choosing the holiday of a lifetime'.*

I then worked with the AI to scope my 'holiday of a lifetime' decision, as detailed in the following appendices:

- **Appendix 1b** shows how Google Gemini summarised the **Decision Scoping** conversation that led to my own specific holiday of a lifetime brief.

- **Appendix 1c** gives a copy of the final **Decision Brief** itself.

Should you wish, you can use the same decision-specific prompt to decide on your own 'holiday of a lifetime'. While the results will be unique to you, this will allow you to compare both your process and outcomes with mine. Alternatively, use the same process for any high-impact, high-complexity decision of your choice.

Decision Scoping - Conclusion

Decision Scoping, leading to a well-crafted **Decision Brief**, fundamentally transforms the decision-making process by establishing clear boundaries, focus and purpose. More than just documentation, it serves as a strategic compass that guides organisations through complexity while preventing common decision-making pitfalls.

The most successful decision briefs achieve three critical balances. First, they precisely define the decision's scope—neither too narrow to miss strategic opportunities nor too broad to become unactionable. Second, they establish clear evaluation criteria that protect against both premature convergence and endless deliberation. Third, they identify the essential work required for informed decision-making without slipping into analysis paralysis.

Organisations typically stumble at this stage in predictable ways. Many rush to solutions before properly defining the problem, a tendency the structured divergent-convergent approach directly counters by forcing disciplined thinking about what decision truly needs to be made. Others create overly vague decision statements that try to please everyone but ultimately provide insufficient direction. Some briefs fail to establish meaningful acceptance criteria, making it impossible to objectively evaluate the eventual decision. The process outlined in this chapter specifically addresses these common pitfalls.

The **Decision Brief** creates the foundation upon which all subsequent phases build. When you enter the **Decision Preparation** phase, the clarity established in your brief will focus your information gathering, prevent scope creep and ensure you're solving the right problem. This foundation dramatically increases the likelihood of reaching decisions that are not just faster, but genuinely smarter and better.

AI augmentation enhances this process in ways traditional approaches cannot match. It systematically explores alternative problem framings that might not occur to human decision-makers, surfaces non-obvious perspectives that challenge conventional thinking and helps identify implicit assumptions that often remain hidden. The partnership between human insight and AI's analytical capabilities creates decision briefs that are more thorough, balanced and robust than either could achieve alone.

Before moving to **Decision Preparation**, confirm you've completed these essential elements:

- ☐ The decision definition is clear, specific, and agreed upon by all key stakeholders.

- ☐ Acceptance criteria are comprehensive, measurable and aligned with organisational objectives.

- ☐ Required preparation work is clearly identified and appropriately scoped.

- ☐ Key constraints and boundaries have been explicitly documented.

- ☐ Stakeholder perspectives have been considered in framing the decision.

- ☐ The brief has been reviewed for hidden assumptions or biases.

- ☐ The completed brief has been properly documented and shared as appropriate.

With this comprehensive foundation established, you're now ready to move to the **Decision Preparation** phase, where you'll systematically build the knowledge base needed to make an informed decision. The clarity and focus established in your brief will guide this next crucial phase of work, ensuring your preparation efforts remain targeted on what truly matters for making a faster, smarter, better decision.

CHAPTER 6: Decision Preparation

Introduction & overview

Your decision has been scoped and your **Decision Brief** is now written. It defines the decision, sets out work you need to do in the remaining four phases of AI-augmented decisions and proposes acceptance criteria for evaluating your decision, once made. You are now ready to move to Phase 2: **Decision Preparation**.

The need for effective preparation

Every significant organisational decision needs to be underpinned with knowledge and understanding. Yet, in today's data-rich environment, the challenge isn't usually finding information - it's knowing what information matters, how to interpret it meaningfully and when to stop gathering more. Regardless of what type of organisation you are in and the decision you are making (and even if you are an individual pursuing the holiday of a lifetime!) the fundamental challenge remains the same: how do we build a sufficient knowledge base for decision-making without falling into 'analysis paralysis'?

Good preparation is essential for good decisions, and this is where many organisations struggle. Some gather endless data without moving toward actual decisions. Others rush through with insufficient analysis, relying too heavily on intuition, past experience or the HIPPO – Highest Paid Person's Opinion.[89] The key is finding the right balance - being thorough enough to understand the complexity of your decision while maintaining momentum toward actually making it.

Balancing thoroughness and progress

This challenge is particularly acute in the context of AI-augmented decision-making. AI tools give us unprecedented ability to process and analyse information, but this capability can be both a blessing and a curse. While AI can help us uncover insights we might otherwise miss, it can also tempt us to endlessly explore new data angles or analysis paths.

This chapter, and the super-prompt in Appendix 2a, provide a structured approach to **Decision Preparation** that works across different types of decision and different organisational contexts. Whether your success metrics are financial returns or social impact, whether your stakeholders are shareholders or service beneficiaries, the principles and practices outlined here will help you gather and analyse the right information to support your decision-making process.

A structured approach to Decision Preparation

Your objective for **Decision Preparation** is straightforward. You are setting out to get everything prepared so you can move on to make the decision in Phase 3 of our 5-phase process, the **Decision-Making Workshop**. However, achieving this objective in a way that truly supports faster, smarter, better decisions requires a systematic approach that balances comprehensive exploration with focused analysis.

The approach presented in this chapter, and detailed as guidance for your AI in the super-prompt in Appendix 2a, is designed to adapt to different organisational contexts while providing a clear structure that prevents common preparation pitfalls. It draws on proven practices from decision science while incorporating AI capabilities that enhance traditional information gathering and analysis.

Key challenges in Decision Preparation

There are several fundamental challenges to doing **Decision Preparation** well:

1. **Decision landscape challenge:** The decision landscape is the domain or territory within which your eventual decision will lie. The challenge is to ensure that the landscape you consider includes all possible viable decision candidates whilst usefully excluding those that are beyond its boundaries.

2. **Information and insight challenge:** Given this decision landscape, what data, arguments and insights need to be mined within it to i) allow critical comparison between decision candidates, ii) identify new candidates that may have been omitted and iii) ultimately differentiate between your chosen set of candidates to evaluate whether your preferred decision is good enough? This information needs to be systematically gathered and recorded to allow trade-offs to be made and a final decision candidate to be chosen in the next phase of decision-making.

3. **Complexity challenge:** High-impact, high-complexity decisions, by their very nature, are influenced by a multitude of factors and, in turn, influence a multitude of other factors. Your preparation, therefore, needs to cast a wide net. Casting this net too wide, however, leads to analysis paralysis: an endless loop of research that keeps begging more and more questions and never gets us any closer to decision-making. Cast the net in the wrong place and you over-prepare for the decision you don't make and under-prepare for the decision you do make. You might, for example, prepare diligently for what you expect to be a financial decision only for it to turn out that the key decision is all to do with marketing and sales (which has financial implications but these are follow-on consequences, not the key decision).

Done well, **Decision Preparation** adequately informs the decision-makers of both the complexity of the decision they are about to make and the foreseeable implications of the options they have to decide between.

Decision Preparation – the process

To make **Decision Preparation** less likely to be rendered irrelevant you will organise this phase of work around a set of 'decision candidates' – a set of possible options for the decision you will eventually make. To ensure you cast the net wide, whilst also avoiding analysis paralysis, you will be guided through a rigorous process designed to encourage divergent thinking followed by convergent thinking, just like you did in **Decision Scoping**.

Decision Preparation begins with divergent research and exploration, identifying a diverse array of potential decision candidates across different categories and approaches, based on the **Decision Brief**. We develop multiple lenses through which to compare and evaluate these options - these 'decision differentiators' are used to differentiate the decision candidates in terms of the value they deliver, the costs they incur, the risks they involve and impacts they have on stakeholders for the organisation making the decision. The exploration of the 'decision landscape' continues to identify commonalities, clusters and new candidates that may have been missed.

Convergent thinking then helps us refine this wealth of information, narrowing the set of viable decision candidates to those most worthy of detailed consideration. This involves bringing together, combining and synthesising multiple ideas into something more cohesive and actionable. We prioritise the most relevant differentiators for comparing options in this specific context and synthesise all these elements into a coherent set of decision candidates and the means of assessing them that will effectively guide the upcoming **Decision-Making Workshop**.

We then seek further context for decision-making by systematically gathering relevant information on the narrowed set of decision candidates and their differentiators. These data and insights are recorded, along with descriptions of the candidates and differentiators already identified, to fully inform and facilitate decision-making in the next phase.

Decision candidates will be devised and contextualised by means of the six discrete activities described below.

Activity #1 - Exploring decision candidates

This first activity uses divergent thinking to identify and expand the range of potential decisions ('decision candidates') that could address the needs defined in the **Decision Brief**. The aim is to generate a broad set of possibilities, exploring variations (extreme, subtle, time-based, stakeholder-focused), hybrid approaches, opposite thinking and resource-shifted scenarios, without premature evaluation. We seek a broad range to ensure promising options aren't overlooked.

Activity #2 - Identifying decision differentiators

Next, again using divergent thinking, you explore the factors ('decision differentiators') that will be used to compare and evaluate the candidates. This involves identifying a wide range of potential value (financial, stakeholder, experiential), costs (direct, indirect, opportunity, implementation), risks (implementation, external, performance, scalability, opportunity), and stakeholder impacts (primary / secondary, internal / external, winners / losers, influence / interest) across different time horizons to create a robust framework for later assessment. These decision differentiators should be consistent with the acceptance criteria recorded previously in the **Decision Brief**.

Activity #3 - Exploring the decision landscape

This activity shifts to reflective exploration, bringing together the candidates and differentiators identified so far to understand the overall shape of the potential decision space. You look for commonalities, fundamental differences and potential clusters among the candidates based on shared features (e.g. value, approach, scale, risk profile). This mapping exercise helps identify any overlooked possibilities or obvious gaps in the emerging decision space before moving to convergence.

Activity #4 - Narrowing the consideration set

This activity uses convergent thinking to narrow down the broad set of decision candidates and differentiators: candidates may be removed (e.g. infeasible, out of scope), combined or sharpened; differentiators are prioritised based on relevance to the specific decision and key trade-offs. This results in a focused set of well-defined decision candidates and the means for assessing them, ready for the **Decision-Making Workshop**.

Activity #5 - Information gathering

This activity uses a systematic framework to gather contextual information from a variety of sources, relevant to the selected set of decision candidates and differentiators, to inform decision-making in the **Decision-Making Workshop**. Some of that information will come from data – product/service data, market data, financial data. Some will come from people – your front-line teams, managers and partner/supplier organisations. Some may come from exploring the web or finding research reports.

Activity #6 – Producing a Record of Decision Preparation

This final activity brings together all the relevant information from the **Decision Preparation** phase of the decision-making process to produce a final record of the selected decision candidates, the prioritised differentiators associated with them, the rationale behind their selection, any proposed changes to the **Decision Brief** and a record of the information gathered for each decision candidate.

This systematic progression through divergent exploration, landscape mapping and convergent refinement ensures that **Decision Preparation** is both thorough and focused, building a solid foundation for the next phase, the **Decision-Making Workshop**.

AI-augmenting the Decision Preparation process

Artificial intelligence transforms **Decision Preparation** from a potentially overwhelming data-gathering exercise into a structured, insight-rich process. Rather than simply accelerating traditional research methods, AI serves as a thinking partner, augmenting each of the six activities as guided by the super-prompt (Appendix 2a). It helps manage the core challenge of balancing thoroughness with progress, preventing analysis paralysis by structuring exploration and ensuring insights lead towards decision-making.

1. Enhancing decision candidate exploration

AI excels at expanding the range of potential decision candidates, providing value in several key ways:

- **Systematic candidate generation:** AI can methodically identify a comprehensive set of decision candidates by analysing the decision definition from multiple angles and perspectives.

- **Pattern recognition across precedents:** AI can rapidly analyse similar decisions made by other organisations, identifying patterns of success and failure that might inform new options.

- **Lateral thinking support:** Beyond conventional alternatives, AI can generate innovative hybrid approaches by combining elements from different decision candidates in non-obvious ways, perhaps prompting exploration of 'opposites' or contradicting conventional wisdom.

- **Assumption challenging:** AI can systematically identify and question the underlying assumptions behind each potential decision, revealing blind spots and expanding the solution space.

2. Strengthening decision differentiator development

AI augmentation significantly enhances how organisations evaluate different decision candidates:

- **Multi-dimensional analysis:** AI can simultaneously evaluate decision candidates across numerous criteria, creating nuanced comparisons that capture complexity better than simple pros and cons lists.

- **Impact modelling:** AI can help forecast the potential consequences of different decisions across various timeframes and stakeholder groups, providing a more comprehensive view of likely outcomes.

- **Risk identification:** Beyond highlighting obvious risks, AI can detect subtle patterns of potential challenges by analysing historical cases and system interactions, prompting consideration across diverse categories like implementation, external factors, performance and scalability.

- **Value alignment assessment:** AI can evaluate how different decision candidates align with organisational values and strategic priorities, ensuring considerations beyond purely operational factors, potentially exploring different facets of value such as financial, stakeholder or experiential.

3. Deepening decision landscape exploration

AI fundamentally transforms how organisations synthesise **Decision Preparation** into actionable knowledge:

- **Information synthesis:** AI can integrate disparate inputs into coherent decision landscapes that represent the full complexity of the decision context while remaining accessible to decision-makers.

- **Visual representation:** AI can help visualise complex decision landscapes by making relationships between decision candidates, criteria and stakeholders more intuitively understandable.

- **Insight surfacing:** Beyond merely organising information, AI can highlight non-obvious patterns and connections that might otherwise remain hidden in the volume of preparation materials, facilitating exploration of commonalities, fundamental differences and potential clusters among candidates to reveal the overall shape of the decision space and identify potential gaps.

4. Guiding the narrowing of the consideration set

During this convergent phase, AI ensures the outputs are clear, concise and comprehensive:

- **Information synthesis:** AI assists in refining the broad set of candidates and differentiators explored earlier. It helps combine, sharpen or synthesise options, identifying redundancies or infeasible candidates based on scope or constraints defined in the brief. AI can also help prioritise the most critical differentiators that highlight key trade-offs for this specific decision.

- **Structured convergence:** AI facilitates the process of narrowing options by applying the prioritised differentiators consistently across candidates. It ensures the final selected set is manageable, well-defined, diverse where appropriate (e.g. balancing financial vs. stakeholder focus), and that the assessment criteria are clear, feasible and directly aligned with the **Decision Brief**. AI can also check if insights gained during preparation necessitate revisions to the original **Decision Brief**.

5. Accelerating information gathering

AI significantly accelerates and enhances the systematic gathering of relevant information needed to evaluate the narrowed set of decision candidates against the prioritised differentiators:

- **Framework adherence:** AI helps maintain focus by structuring the information gathering according to the defined framework (e.g. ensuring data is collected for each candidate against each key differentiator). This ensures an evidence-base is built systematically to facilitate comparison and evaluation in the next phase.

- **Source identification and retrieval:** AI can rapidly identify potential internal and external information sources (databases, reports, expert repositories, web sources, research papers) relevant to specific candidates and differentiators. Where access permits, it can assist in retrieving and summarising key data and insights, including both quantitative and qualitative information.

- **Insight extraction and gap analysis:** AI can process large volumes of text and data to extract pertinent facts, identify conflicting information, surface underlying assumptions and highlight potential trade-offs. It can also help identify gaps in the information gathered, suggesting areas where further investigation might be needed to ensure a balanced view across all candidates.

6. Documenting Decision Preparation

AI streamlines the final activity of consolidating all outputs from the **Decision Preparation** phase into a comprehensive and coherent record:

- **Structured compilation:** AI assists in compiling the full descriptions of the selected decision candidates, the prioritised differentiators, the rationale for their selection and any revisions made to the **Decision Brief** into a single, organised document.

- **Information consolidation:** AI integrates the gathered information, ensuring data, insights, sources, references, key assumptions and identified trade-offs are clearly documented for each candidate in relation to the differentiators.

- **Output generation:** AI helps generate the final '**Record of Decision Preparation**' in a clear, accessible format, ready for use in the subsequent **Decision-Making Workshop**. This ensures all necessary context and evidence is readily available to participants.

The goal of AI augmentation in **Decision Preparation** isn't to automate the process but to make it more thorough, insightful and efficient. By systematically exploring the decision candidates from multiple perspectives, this human-AI partnership helps decision-makers move to the decision-making phase with a richer understanding of possibilities, implications and evaluation approaches. This comprehensive foundation dramatically increases the likelihood of making decisions that are not just faster, but genuinely smarter and better.

Output: Record of Decision Preparation

The primary output from **Decision Preparation** (and hence the input into the **Decision-Making Workshop**) is the '**Record of Decision Preparation**', a document detailing the final, refined set of selected decision candidates and the means of assessing them. This includes a clear definition of each chosen candidate, how they relate to the **Decision Brief** and the prioritised decision differentiators and a framework of contextual information that will be used to move from differentiating decision candidates to deciding upon a single proposed decision in the next phase.

This documentation, informed by the exploration of the decision landscape and resulting from convergent thinking to narrow the consideration set, ensures decision-makers in the workshop can focus on evaluating a well-prepared, manageable, yet diverse set of viable options. The original **Decision Brief** may also need to be updated based on insights gained in the **Decision Preparation** process.

Your instructions for starting Decision Preparation

In the **Decision Scoping** phase (Chapter 5) you and your chosen AI produced a **Decision Brief**. To move forward with the detailed research and analysis needed to make your decision, follow these instructions:

1. Download the **Decision Preparation Super-prompt** (given in **Appendix 2a**) from goalatlas.com/ai-augmented-decisions via the QR code below.

Note: Whilst the purpose of this chapter has been to give you an overview of the process of **Decision Preparation**, you are welcome to read the full **Decision Preparation Super-prompt** in Appendix 2a to understand the specific instructions the AI will be given.

2. Upload this super-prompt to a new session in your AI platform, along with your **Decision Brief** from the previous phase.

3. Type in the following prompt:

    I have just uploaded the Decision Preparation Super-prompt. I would like you to work through the process specified in this document. The decision I'd like you to apply this process to is defined in the Decision Brief that I have also uploaded. As you work through the process, please use the Decision Brief to inform, shape and support your decision preparation.

The AI will then guide you through an extensive **Decision Preparation** conversation for the specific decision you are working on. At the end of that conversation, you will be prompted to download or copy-and-save the resulting '**Record of Decision Preparation**' for use in the next phase. This document, which will be used to inform decision-making in the **Decision-**

Making Workshop, contains:

- full descriptions of the selected decision candidates;
- the prioritised differentiators associated with these candidates;
- the rationale behind candidate selection;
- any proposed changes to the Decision Brief;
- a record of the information gathered for each selected decision candidate, along with references, key assumptions and potential trade-offs.

An example of AI-augmented Decision Preparation

As you saw in **Decision Scoping**, we are using the case study of 'choosing the holiday of a lifetime' as a tangible example of the principles of decision-making applied to a relatively complex, but readily understood, real-world decision.

Following the instructions above (using Google Gemini 2.5 Pro), I moved from the **Decision Brief** produced in the **Decision Scoping** phase to the detailed research and analysis needed as preparation for actually making my 'holiday of a lifetime' decision, as documented in the following appendices:

- **Appendix 2b** shows how Google Gemini summarised the **Decision Preparation** conversation for my own 'holiday of a lifetime' decision.

- **Appendix 2c** gives a copy of the final '**Record of Decision Preparation**' for this conversation, bringing together all the relevant information on my selected decision candidates.

Should you wish, you can continue to work through your own unique version of this 'choosing the holiday of a lifetime' decision and compare your process and outcomes with mine. Alternatively, use the same process for any high-impact, high-complexity decision of your choice.

Decision Preparation - Conclusion

Decision Preparation forms the critical bridge between defining what needs to be decided and actually making that decision. As this chapter has demonstrated, preparation doesn't simply involve gathering information—it requires building a structured understanding of your decision landscape that encompasses possible alternatives, differentiating factors and data / insights from a broad range of information sources. When done well, this phase creates the essential underpinning knowledge for confident, well-informed decision-making.

The most effective **Decision Preparation** achieves two crucial balances. It explores a diverse range of decision candidates while maintaining focus on those that truly address the core challenges identified in your brief. It examines multiple differentiating factors without getting lost in analysis paralysis.

Organisations frequently encounter several pitfalls during **Decision Preparation**. Some gather endless data without moving toward actionable insights, becoming trapped in an ever-expanding research phase. Others rush through with superficial analysis, relying too heavily on preconceptions or limited perspectives. Many fail to adequately consider the human and organisational dynamics that will ultimately determine whether a decision can be successfully adopted. The structured approach outlined in this chapter - with its deliberate movement through six activities encompassing divergent exploration, landscape mapping, convergent refinement, information gathering and recording - directly addresses these common challenges.

The decision candidates (and their means of assessment) documented in this phase transform subsequent decision-making by providing a comprehensive yet navigable map of possibilities, constraints and evaluation criteria. This enables decision-makers to see connections and patterns that might otherwise remain hidden, and it ensures that important factors aren't overlooked in the pressure of decision-making moments. This foundation dramatically increases the likelihood that your organisation will identify genuinely innovative solutions rather than defaulting to the most obvious alternatives.

AI augmentation particularly enhances **Decision Preparation** by rapidly analysing complex information from multiple sources, identifying non-obvious relationships between different decision factors and generating innovative hybrid options that might not occur to human analysts. It helps organisations by providing a consistent structure for evaluating diverse options against multiple criteria. This human-AI partnership creates a preparation output that is both more comprehensive and more insightful than traditional approaches could achieve.

Before moving to the **Decision-Making Workshop** phase, verify you've completed these essential elements:

☐ A diverse set of potential decision candidates has been explored and a refined set documented.

☐ There are a manageable number of decision candidates in this final consideration set.

☐ A broad range of potential decision differentiators has been explored and a prioritised set selected to compare candidate decisions.

☐ The decision landscape (commonalities, differences, clusters) has been explored to inform refinement.

☐ Contextual information relating to the candidates and their differentiators has been gathered and recorded to support decision-making.

☐ The brief has been reviewed and revised where appropriate.

☐ The final set of decision candidates and means of assessment have been documented and shared as appropriate.

With this comprehensive preparation established through a structured, AI-augmented process, you're now prepared to enter the **Decision-Making Workshop** phase with confidence. The structured exploration and refinement you've completed provide the necessary context, options and evaluation criteria for a focused, productive decision-making process that can deliver genuinely better outcomes.

CHAPTER 7: Decision-Making Workshop

Introduction & overview

The transition from **Decision Preparation** to active decision-making represents a crucial pivot point in the overall AI-augmented decisions process. Whilst preparation focuses on building comprehensive underpinning knowledge and analysis, decision-making centres on the collaborative work of evaluating options, debating alternatives and ultimately reaching a formal **Decision Proposal**. This shift demands a careful balance between maintaining the momentum built during preparation while ensuring sufficient space for thorough deliberation.

At the heart of effective decision-making lies the structured **Decision-Making Workshop**. Research suggests three key advantages to using workshops to make important organisational decisions: [90]

1. collective ownership and commitment;

2. enhanced quality of the solution;

3. improved organisational health and agility.

Focused workshop sessions bring together key participants to transform prepared insights into a proposed decision. However, workshops must be more than just allocated time for discussion - they require careful design, preparation and skilled facilitation. The process outlined here, designed to be augmented by AI following the detailed **Decision-Making Workshop Super-prompt** in Appendix 3a, creates an environment where participants can fully assimilate complex information, challenge assumptions productively and work toward clear conclusions. Establishing psychological safety[91] is paramount; workshop leaders should ensure that:

*   all voices will be heard – one way to achieve this is to be clear that the conversation will respect 'equity of voice' – everyone will be expected to talk for a similar amount of time;

*   all contributions will be valued;

*   all knowledge and experience will be respected;

*   all judgement will be focused on the ideas being discussed, not the

individuals discussing them;

- all criticism will be constructive.

A critical success factor in these workshops is the balance between **divergent** and **convergent** thinking.

Divergent thinking encourages full exploration of each decision candidate's implications, strengths and limitations. Participants generate potential hybrid approaches by combining elements from different options, consider multiple perspectives on how each option might perform against criteria and identify various adoption approaches along with potential challenges. This ensures that options are fully explored and that premature consensus doesn't lead to suboptimal decisions.

Convergent thinking then guides participants toward a proposed decision through systematic evaluation of options against established criteria. Options may be eliminated or combined to focus on the most promising approaches as consensus builds around the optimal decision given available information. The process culminates in the articulation of clear reasoning for the proposed decision, including the key factors that influenced the choice and why this option best satisfies the acceptance criteria established in the Decision Brief. It drives the decision-makers toward clear choices and actionable outcomes.

Managing the tension between divergent and convergent thinking requires both structural elements in the workshop design (as detailed below) and skilled, objective facilitation during the session itself - where the facilitator remains neutral about the decision outcome while ensuring the decision-making process is robust.

Preparing for the Workshop: Design and Pre-Workshop Briefing

Before the **Decision-Making Workshop** convenes, careful preparation is essential to design the decision-making process and make sure all workshop participants are briefed on what to expect in the workshop.

Producing a Pre-Workshop Briefing Document

The first requirement for this phase of work is the production of a **Pre-Workshop Briefing Document**. Its purpose is to ensure all participants arrive at the workshop fully informed and ready to engage effectively, saving valuable discussion time. This typically includes six elements, the first of which are:

1. **Decision definition & context**
   A clear statement of the decision to be made (from the **Decision Brief**, potentially updated), why it matters, and links to relevant background information.

2. **Decision candidates & means of assessment**
   The potential options identified and refined during **Decision Preparation**, along with the agreed methods for evaluating them (from the **Record of Decision Preparation** from the previous phase).

3. **Decision acceptance criteria**
   The criteria (from the **Decision Brief**, potentially updated) against which the final decision will be judged.

Added to this we need to define the 'who', 'when' and 'how' of the workshop itself. Let's work through who is involved and what their responsibilities are, the workshop timetable and the methods and techniques to be used in the workshop:

4. **Workshop participants – roles and responsibilities**
   A clear delineation of roles is vital for an effective workshop. Five key roles need to be clearly defined in the briefing document:

   a. **Decision Owners:** Those with the formal authority to commit the organisation to the decision and with ultimate accountability for that decision and its outcomes. They are the core decision-makers.

   b. **Stakeholders:** Individuals or teams significantly affected by the decision or key to its adoption. Some may be decision-makers, others provide input.

   c. **Subject Matter Experts (SMEs):** Specialists providing critical knowledge. They inform the decision but are not typically decision-makers. Their input might be via written submissions, presentations or Q&A sessions.

   d. **Facilitators:** Neutral guides of the workshop process, ensuring it stays on track and adheres to agreed principles (like equity of voice). Facilitators can be internal or external.

   e. **AI-Leads:** The individual or team interacting with the AI to provide real-time information, analysis and documentation support during the workshop. This function might be performed by someone also holding another role (e.g. a stakeholder or SME).

The core decision-making group (primarily Decision Owners, potentially key Stakeholders) should ideally be limited to 5-7 members to balance diverse perspectives with effective interaction. Larger groups may require additional structures to ensure all voices are heard.

5. **Workshop timetable and pacing**
   The duration and pacing of the workshop require careful thought. How much time is needed? Should it be a single intensive day or spread over multiple sessions?

   While a single-day workshop can work for well-prepared decisions, high-impact, high-complexity choices often benefit from multiple sessions spread over days or weeks (e.g. Session 1, for context and exploration, followed by an analysis period before Session 2, for deliberation and decision formation). This allows for reflection, deeper analysis and consultation, often saving time over the longer term by improving decision quality and adoption readiness.

6. **Workshop processes and tools**
   The specific processes and tools that will be employed during the workshop to structure discussion and analysis effectively will ideally be identified in advance. These range from SWOT analysis or multi-criteria decision analysis for assessing decision candidates to pre-mortem analysis for identifying hypothetical threats and weaknesses for risk evaluation. The **Pre-Workshop Briefing Document** needs to be clear about a set of proposed tools and processes whilst indicating flexibility to adapt the proposal as the workshop proceeds.

Once these elements have been considered, the **Pre-Workshop Briefing Document** can be compiled. It should be a concise yet sufficiently comprehensive summary of:

1. The decision definition & context;

2. The decision candidates & means of assessment;

3. The decision acceptance criteria;

4. Workshop participants, including their roles and responsibilities;

5. Workshop timetable;

6. Workshop processes and tools to be used.

This briefing document can then be circulated to workshop participants in advance of the **Decision-Making Workshop**.

The Decision-Making Workshop structure and process

With preparation complete and participants briefed, the workshop itself convenes. It follows a structured four-activity format designed to move from a shared understanding of the decision to be made to a formal **Decision Proposal**. This structure is designed to ensure both divergent exploration and convergent focus:

Activity #1: Introduction and context-setting

- **Purpose:** Before diving into options, ensure shared understanding of the specific decision to be made and alignment with why it matters to the organisation and what challenge it aims to address.

- **Key Actions:** Review the decision definition, scope and importance; confirm acceptance criteria and constraints (budget, timeline); establish workshop process, roles and decision-making mechanism (e.g. consensus, vote); align on expected outcomes.

- **Thinking Mode:** Primarily convergent, ensuring everyone is on the same page.

Activity #2: Exploration of decision candidates

- **Purpose:** Thoroughly understand each potential option before evaluation.

- **Key Actions:** Systematically present each decision candidate and their differentiators; surface strengths, limitations and assumptions; encourage participants to add perspectives; identify potential hybrid approaches by combining elements; address clarifying questions.

- **Thinking Mode:** Primarily divergent, opening up possibilities and understanding.

Activity #3: Analysis & deliberation

- **Purpose:** Rigorously evaluate the viable options against agreed criteria.

- **Key Actions:** Apply agreed evaluation frameworks (e.g. decision matrices, cost-benefit analysis); actively challenge assumptions (using techniques like pre-mortem analysis or devil's advocacy); consider adoption implications (resources, readiness, risks); systematically compare options against criteria and differentiators.

- **Thinking Mode**: Mix of divergent (challenging, exploring implications) and convergent (evaluating against criteria).

Activity #4: Decision formation

- **Purpose:** Synthesise the analysis and arrive at a proposed decision.

- **Key Actions:** Consolidate key findings and insights; apply the predetermined decision mechanism (e.g. facilitated consensus, voting); clearly articulate the proposed decision; document the rationale, key influencing factors, trade-offs accepted and any significant dissenting views.

- **Thinking Mode:** Primarily convergent, driving towards a specific choice.

AI-augmenting the Decision-Making Workshop

Throughout both the preparation and the live workshop activities, AI serves as a powerful augmentation tool. As always, its role is not to make decisions but to enhance human decision-making.

Pre-workshop preparation

AI can help in designing the workshop and producing the pre-workshop briefing in three key ways. Firstly, it can help assimilate all the documentation that has been produced so far, such as the **Decision Brief** from **Decision Scoping** and the '**Record of Decision Preparation**' (which sets out the decision candidates and the means of differentiating them). Secondly, it can help work through, and challenge, the design decisions for the workshop. Are the right people involved and have they been given the right roles? Does the workshop timetable give enough time for meaningful and decisive discussion, whilst maintaining momentum? Are the proposed tools and processes for the workshop the best ones, given the specific decision being considered, the people involved and the timetable? Thirdly it can help assimilate this information to produce the **Pre-Workshop Briefing Document**, ensuring its content is concise yet sufficiently comprehensive.

During the Decision-Making Workshop

A key issue to be resolved with the decision-makers and workshop facilitator is the extent to which AI is to be used during the **Decision-Making Workshop**. Broadly, there are three possibilities:

1. **Not at all.** AI's role is limited to preparing for the workshop (including producing the **Pre-Workshop Briefing Document**) and then following up on the workshop discussions.

2. **Intermittently.** Typically during breaks in the workshop timetable or at specific moments when AI can help answer a specific question or rapidly produce additional background information.

3. **Always-on throughout the workshop.** Clearly, if the workshop is being recorded or is happening online, AI could give live summaries, instant feedback on issues discussed and alerts if key issues are missed. A more common use-case is where a person is assigned to be the AI-Lead, working with the AI in the background, allowing the discussion to flow without interruption. Whenever the AI comes up with anything of value to add to the discussion, the AI-Lead can quietly pass it to the workshop facilitator to be introduced into the workshop discussions.

During the workshop, the AI can transform from a preparation tool into an active support system for decision-making. It can serve as a real-time knowledge base, capable of instantly retrieving relevant supporting data or answering specific questions about the evidence base. This capability helps keep discussions focused and productive – rather than spending time hunting through documents for relevant information, participants can immediately access the data they need to move discussions forward.

As the workshop moves towards an actual decision, AI's analytical and simulation capabilities come to the fore, rapidly assessing individual ideas or comparing multiple ideas. With the right information available to it, an AI can help evaluate resource implications, identify potential unintended consequences and assess risks. This real-time analysis helps decision-makers refine options with a clearer understanding of their implications.

As decisions begin to form, an AI can assist in capturing not just the decisions themselves but the rich context around them. It can document key discussion points and rationale, test emerging decisions against predefined criteria and begin identifying potential adoption challenges. This comprehensive documentation proves invaluable both for immediate next steps and for future organisational learning.

Key principle for successful augmentation of decision-making using AI

Crucially, an AI must *inform*, not *decide*. Human judgment remains central. The AI should handle routine analysis and surface non-obvious insights, freeing participants for strategic thinking. Its use should be inclusive and transparent, enhancing rather than directing the human dynamics of the workshop. **Note my disclaimer at the front of this book:**

> *"...this book is all about using AI to enable humans to make faster, smarter, better decisions, not for AI to make the decisions on our behalf.*
>
> *DECISION-MAKING IS ALWAYS THE RESPONSIBILITY OF HUMANS. AIs MAKE ASSUMPTIONS AND MISTAKES – ALWAYS DOUBLE CHECK THEIR RESPONSES.*
>
> *The use of AI tools can also introduce new types of data security issues, not necessarily raised by other types of technology. Before using any of the AI techniques described in this book, please make sure you are acting in compliance with your own organisation's AI policies and standards. If you don't have any such policies and standards, guidance on data and security issues can be found from the National Cyber-Security Centre in the USA[92] or from the Information Commissioner's Office in the UK."* [93]

Output: The Decision Proposal

The primary output of the **Decision-Making Workshop** is a formal **Decision Proposal**. This document captures not just what was decided but also the why and the how. It serves multiple critical purposes: providing transparency, creating organisational memory, forming the basis for the next phase (**Decision Validation**) and guiding eventual adoption.

A comprehensive **Decision Proposal,** often drafted with AI assistance based on the workshop discussions and adhering to best practices outlined in the **Decision-Making Workshop Super-prompt**, typically includes:

1. **Proposed decision statement:** A clear, specific statement of the recommended decision, including any qualifiers or conditions.

2. **Context, background and options considered:** A summary of the original decision need, the process followed (including Decision Preparation), the final candidates evaluated in the workshop and potentially why others were eliminated earlier.

3. **How the decision was made:** An overview of the workshop process, the evaluation methods used, key data and evidence considered, primary factors influencing the choice and the level of consensus reached.

4. **Implications of the decision made:** Critical assumptions made, alignment with organisational goals, expected benefits/value, potential risks or unintended consequences identified and anticipated stakeholder impacts.

5. **Decision process documentation:** Key logistics (when, where), participants and roles and references to supporting documents generated during the workshop.

This document should balance comprehensiveness with clarity, providing enough detail for understanding while remaining accessible. It is typically shared with workshop participants for review before moving to Phase 4: **Decision Validation**.

Your instructions for the Decision-Making Workshop

In the **Decision Scoping** phase (Chapter 5) you and your chosen AI produced a **Decision Brief**. Then, in the **Decision Preparation** phase (Chapter 6) you produced a **Record of Decision Preparation**. To move forward to the decision-making phase, follow these instructions:

1. Download the **Decision-Making Workshop Super-prompt** (given in **Appendix 3a**) from goalatlas.com/ai-augmented-decisions via the QR code below.

   Note: Whilst the purpose of this chapter has been to give you an overview of the **Decision-Making Workshop** structure and process, you are welcome to read the full **Decision-Making Workshop Super-prompt** in Appendix 3a to understand the specific instructions the AI will be given.

2. Upload this super-prompt to a new session in your AI platform, along with the **Record of Decision Preparation** produced in the preceding phases.

3. Type in the following prompt:

   I have just uploaded a Decision-Making Workshop Super-prompt. I would like you to work through the process specified in this document. The decision I'd like you to apply this process to is defined in the Record of Decision Preparation, which I have also uploaded.

The AI will then guide you through the following two stages:

i. The production of a **Pre-Workshop Briefing Document** to ensure all Workshop participants are fully prepared. This will include your inputs to decide on the Workshop participants, their roles and responsibilities, the Workshop timetable and the Workshop processes and tools to be used. Once completed, the **Pre-Workshop Briefing Document** should be circulated to all Workshop participants.

ii.   The **Decision-Making Workshop** itself. This consists of four activities: introduction and context-setting, exploration of the decision options, analysis and deliberation, and finally, forming the decision. The extent to which AI is to be used during the live **Decision-Making Workshop** (not at all / intermittently / always-on) must be agreed with the decision-makers and workshop facilitator prior to the workshop.

At the end of the **Decision-Making Workshop** you will have a formal **Decision Proposal**, which you will be prompted to download or copy-and-save for use in the next phase, **Decision Validation**.

An example of an AI-augmented Decision-Making Workshop

We are using the case study of 'choosing the holiday of a lifetime' to apply the principles of decision-making to a relatively complex, but readily understood, real-world decision.

Following the instructions above, I conducted my own **Decision-Making Workshop** on my 'holiday of a lifetime' decision, with four participants and facilitated using Google Gemini 2.5 Pro, as detailed in the following appendices:

• **Appendix 3b** shows how Google Gemini summarised the **Decision-Making Workshop** for my own 'holiday of a lifetime' decision.

• **Appendix 3c** gives a copy of my final **Decision Proposal**.

Should you wish, you can continue to work through your own unique version of this 'choosing the holiday of a lifetime' decision and compare your process and outcomes with mine. Alternatively, use the same process for any high-impact, high-complexity decision of your choice.

Decision-Making Workshop - Conclusion

The **Decision-Making Workshop** serves as the crucial engine of Phase 3, transforming the structured analysis and prepared options from Phase 2 into a concrete, well-reasoned **Decision Proposal**. This collaborative forum is where insights are debated, assumptions are challenged and collective judgment is applied to navigate complexity and arrive at a specific course of action. Successfully executing this phase bridges the gap between understanding the decision landscape and committing to a path forward.

The most effective decision-making workshops achieve several critical balances. They meticulously follow a structured process - encompassing thorough preparation, distinct activities (context-setting, exploration, analysis, formation) and clearly defined roles - whilst retaining the flexibility to adapt to the conversation's flow. They skilfully manage the inherent tension between divergent thinking (fully exploring options and implications) and convergent thinking (systematically evaluating and narrowing choices). Furthermore, they foster psychological safety, ensuring all voices are heard and valued, and integrate the AI-Lead role thoughtfully to support, not dominate, the human-centric deliberation process.

Organisations frequently stumble during this phase in predictable ways. Insufficient preparation or poorly crafted briefing documents can lead to wasted time and unfocused discussions. Ambiguity in roles or poor decision-making mechanisms can cause confusion and hinder progress. Perhaps most commonly, workshops may fail to effectively navigate the divergent-convergent cycle, either rushing to premature conclusions or getting bogged down in endless debate without clear criteria for resolution. The structured four-activity approach outlined in this chapter ('Introduction and context-setting', 'Exploration of decision candidates', 'Analysis & deliberation' and 'Decision formation') and an emphasis on clear roles, pre-workshop briefing and skilled facilitation directly mitigate these risks.

The **Decision Proposal** generated through this workshop phase significantly enhances the decision's trajectory. By documenting not just the what but the why and how - including the rationale, alternatives considered, key influencing factors, and trade-offs - it provides essential transparency and creates organisational memory. This **Decision Proposal** forms the key input into the subsequent **Decision Validation** phase, increasing the likelihood of robust scrutiny, stakeholder buy-in and, ultimately, successful adoption.

AI augmentation provides powerful leverage throughout this phase. In preparation for the workshop, it aids in assimilating vast amounts of information, challenging workshop design assumptions and efficiently drafting comprehensive briefing documents. During the workshop itself, whether used intermittently or in an 'always-on' capacity via an AI-Lead, it acts as a real-time knowledge base, performs rapid analysis and simulations, helps evaluate options against criteria and assists in meticulously documenting proceedings and the final **Decision Proposal**. This partnership allows human participants to focus their cognitive energy on strategic discussion, critical judgment and nuanced deliberation, ensuring AI informs and enhances, rather than dictates, the decision.

Before moving to **Decision Validation**, confirm you've completed these essential elements:

☐ **Pre-Workshop Briefing Document** distributed and understood by all participants.

☐ Roles (Decision Owners, Stakeholders, SMEs, Facilitator, AI-Lead) clearly defined and assigned.

☐ Workshop adhered to the structured four-activity process (Context, Exploration, Analysis, Formation).

☐ Divergent and convergent thinking were appropriately balanced.

☐ An agreed-upon decision-making mechanism was utilised.

☐ AI augmentation was employed effectively to support, not lead, the process (as applicable).

☐ A comprehensive **Decision Proposal** has been drafted, capturing the decision, rationale, context, implications and process.

☐ The **Decision Proposal** has been reviewed by workshop participants.

With a robust **Decision Proposal** in hand, grounded in thorough preparation and structured deliberation, you are now equipped to proceed to Phase 4: **Decision Validation**. This next phase will rigorously test the proposed decision's soundness and feasibility before final commitment and adoption-planning begin.

CHAPTER 8: Decision Validation

Introduction & overview

After investing significant time and resources in developing a **Decision Proposal**, organisational leaders naturally want to move forward with implementation. However, high-impact, high-complexity decisions deserve one additional step before formal commitment: **Decision Validation**.

Decision Validation aims to strengthen and refine the **Decision Proposal** before committing significant organisational resources to **Decision Adoption**. This phase is not intended to undermine the authority of decision-makers, rather to provide them with additional confidence that their proposed decision remains aligned with their original intentions and is a robust decision, supported by the available evidence. Indeed it is often best to have **Decision Validation** led by the decision-makers.

Decision Validation sets out to answer two core questions:

1. **Is it the right decision?** (Scope Validation)
2. **Is it a justified decision?** (Evidence Validation)

The entire **Decision Validation** process consists of four activities:

Activity #1 - Scope Validation: This activity compares the **Decision Proposal** with the original **Decision Brief** to ensure the proposed solution directly addresses the problem that was set out to be solved.

Activity #2 - Evidence Validation: This activity ensures the rationale within the **Decision Proposal** is demonstrably supported by the research, data and analysis from the **Record of Decision Preparation**.

Activity #3 - Securing decision commitment: This activity focuses on preparing the necessary documentation (the '**Case for the Decision**') to gain formal approval for the decision from the relevant authorities.

Activity #4 - Producing a record of the 'Final Decision': Once the decision is approved, this final activity creates the definitive record that will guide the next phase, **Decision Adoption**.

Decision Validation – the process

Here are these four activities in more detail, as they apply to high-impact, high-complexity decisions:

Activity #1 - Scope Validation

This is the most fundamental validation check. It directly compares the output of the workshop (the **Decision Proposal**) with the original intent (the **Decision Brief**). The key question here is simple: Did we solve the problem we set out to solve?

This involves a straightforward, evidence-based review:

- **Check against decision definition:** Does the proposed decision fall squarely within the scope of the decision as it was defined in the brief? Any deviation here must be deliberate and justified.

- **Check against acceptance criteria:** How does the proposed decision stack up against the specific acceptance criteria defined at the outset? For a business decision, this might mean qualitatively checking a proposed marketing strategy against agreed criteria for brand alignment, market reach, budget adherence, and implementation feasibility. This isn't a re-scoring, but a final confirmation that the choice aligns with the original measures of success.

If the proposal fails to align with the brief, the decision-makers must understand why. It may be that the understanding of the decision evolved for good reason, in which case the **Decision Brief** may need to be formally amended.

Activity #2 - Evidence Validation

Once alignment with the **Decision Brief** is confirmed, the second check ensures the decision is built on a solid foundation of evidence. It asks: *Is the rationale for our decision fully justified by the evidence we gathered?*

This involves tracing the logic from the **Record of Decision Preparation** to the **Decision Proposal**. There are two main aims here:

- **To substantiate key findings:** Are the key claims and conclusions in the proposal—for instance, the scoring of different options—supported by the research data? This means ensuring, for example, that a recommendation to introduce new technology is backed by specific performance data and user feedback documented in the preparation phase.

- **To justify key actions:** If the workshop took a specific action, such as refining an option, is the reason for that action clear from the evidence? A decision to modify a product launch plan, for example, should be directly justified by market research in the **Record of Decision Preparation** that highlighted a potential risk with the original plan.

This check confirms that the decision is not just a product of the workshop's discussion, but a logical conclusion drawn from the preparatory work.

Activity #3 - Securing decision commitment

Once the **Decision Proposal** has been rigorously checked against its original scope and the evidence that supports it, the next activity within the **Decision Validation** phase is to prepare for formal commitment. This is the crucial step where the validated decision moves from a proposal to a committed course of action for the organisation.

This transition typically requires formal approval of the decision by a higher authority, such as a senior executive committee or the Board. Securing this approval is not just a procedural step; it ensures that the organisation's leadership is fully aligned and formally commits the necessary resources and authority for **Decision Adoption**. To achieve this, a clear and compelling **Case for the Decision** must be presented.

A **Case for the Decision** begins by explaining what decision is being presented for approval. What challenge is the organisation facing that necessitates this decision to be made? What is the decision that is being proposed for approval? What benefits should the organisation gain by committing to this decision? Then the decision-validation process is presented. How was the decision scope validated? How was the evidence leading to the decision validated? Was anything raised during this validation that needs addressing? Finally, formal approval for the validated decision is requested, and a record of the approval captured.

Activity #4 - Producing a record of the 'Final Decision'

The final activity of the **Decision Validation** phase is to create the official record of the **Final Decision** that will serve as the primary input for Phase

5: **Decision Adoption**. This is essentially a re-draft of the approved **Case for the Decision** but framed for an audience that will be responsible for adoption rather than approval. The **Final Decision** document should include:

- a statement of final validated decision and the record of its approval (e.g. 'Approved by' / 'Date');

- a summary of the decision context;

- the rationale for the decision;

- key considerations for **Decision Adoption**:

  ◦ key stakeholders;

  ◦ initial thoughts on adoption activities;

  ◦ potential governance or monitoring considerations.

AI-augmenting the Decision Validation process

Artificial intelligence transforms **Decision Validation** from a primarily manual review process into a systematic, comprehensive yet rapid evaluation that can uncover insights and potential issues human reviewers might either overlook or not have time to explore. Rather than replacing human judgment, AI serves as a powerful validation partner that enhances each aspect of the validation process.

To augment the **Scope Validation** phase, an AI can act as a vigilant guardian of the decision's original intent. It can perform a sophisticated semantic comparison between the final **Decision Proposal** and the initial **Decision Brief**, moving beyond simple keyword matching to understand the core concepts and automatically flag any 'scope drift'. As part of this, the AI can audit the proposal against the predefined acceptance criteria, extracting the specific sections that demonstrate compliance and highlighting any criteria that have not been fully addressed. This ensures that the final proposal directly fulfils the goals established at the outset of the process.

For the second activity, **Evidence Validation**, AI can serve as a tireless and objective auditor, ensuring the decision is built on a solid foundation. It can meticulously trace every key assertion in the **Decision Proposal** back to its supporting data within the **Record of Decision Preparation**. This process of claim-to-evidence mapping would highlight any conclusions that are not strongly supported by the evidence. Furthermore, the AI can reconstruct the logical flow of the **Decision-Making Workshop**, creating a 'logic map' to reveal any gaps in reasoning and to verify that any modifications to the plan were clearly justified by the evidence gathered.

Finally, in moving towards decision commitment, AI can significantly accelerate the creation of the high-stakes documentation required for approval by senior leadership or the Board. Most critically, the AI can synthesise all the process outputs into a compelling and comprehensive **Case for the Decision**. This compact document would provide time-poor executives with a persuasive summary of the decision-making journey, the evidence base, and the anticipated benefits, costs, and risks, streamlining the path to formal approval. It can also draft a clear and concise record of the **Final Decision**.

Output: the Final Decision

The final output from **Decision Validation** is the **Final Decision**. This is a minor re-draft of the **Case for the Decision** to make a more effective input into the final phase of AI-augmented decisions, namely **Decision Adoption**. Rather than making the case for decision approval, this new output needs to present the decision as one which has been approved. It needs to pull together all information from previous phases of the process that are relevant to decision adoption. This includes anything to do with decision stakeholders, anything explaining what these stakeholders need to do to adopt the decision and anything to do with how the adoption of this decision is monitored and governed.

Your instructions for starting Decision Validation

In order for **Decision Validation** to rigorously test the **Decision Proposal** you produced in the **Decision-Making Workshop** (in Chapter 7), follow these instructions:

1. Download the **Decision Validation Super-prompt** (given in **Appendix 4a**) from <u>goalatlas.com/ai-augmented-decisions</u> via the QR code below.

Note: Whilst the purpose of this chapter has been to give you an overview of the **Decision Validation** process, you are welcome to read the full **Decision Validation Super-prompt** in Appendix 4a to understand the specific instructions the AI will be following.

2. Upload this super-prompt to a new session in your AI platform, along with your **Decision Proposal** from the previous phase.

3. Type in the following prompt:

   I have just uploaded the Decision Validation Super-prompt. I would like you to work through the process specified in this document. The decision I'd like you to apply this process to is detailed in the Decision Proposal that I have also uploaded.

The AI will then guide you through the four key activities of validation:

i. **Checking the Decision Proposal:** Systematically validating the decision's underlying assumptions, data, and impact against the original brief.

ii. **Adoption Mapping:** Exploring the practical pathways to **Decision Adoption** to identify potential challenges and opportunities.

iii. **Stakeholder Alignment:** Assessing how the decision will be received by key groups to enhance acceptance and effectiveness.

iv. **Moving to decision commitment:** Preparing the documentation needed to get the decision approved by the relevant governing body.

At the end of this process, you will have a validated and finalised decision (the **Final Decision**) which you will be prompted to download or copy-and-save for use in the next phase, **Decision Adoption**.

An example of AI-augmented Decision Validation

We are using the case study of 'choosing the holiday of a lifetime' to apply the principles of decision-making to a relatively complex, but readily understood, real-world decision.

Following the instructions above, I validated my proposed 'holiday of a lifetime' decision, as detailed in the following appendices:

- **Appendix 4b** shows a summary of my **Decision Validation** conversation for the 'holiday of a lifetime' decision, including how the AI raised a critical challenge that strengthened the final choice.

- **Appendix 4c** describes the final output, the **Final Decision**, which formalises the outcome and prepares for the **Decision Adoption** phase.

Should you wish, you can continue to work through your own unique version of this 'choosing the holiday of a lifetime' decision and compare your process and outcomes with mine. Alternatively, use the same process for any high-impact, high-complexity decision of your choice.

Decision Validation - Conclusion

Decision Validation serves as the critical checkpoint between proposing a course of action and committing significant organisational resources to it. This phase ensures that the decision is not only a logical outcome of the preceding workshop but is also robust, evidence-based, and aligned with the original strategic intent. By systematically checking the **Decision Proposal** against both the initial **Decision Brief** and the analytical rigour of the **Record of Decision Preparation**, this phase provides essential confidence and strengthens the final decision before it moves towards **Decision Adoption**. It answers the crucial questions: "Is this the right decision?" and "Is it a justified decision?"

The most effective **Decision Validation** achieves a crucial balance: it is thorough enough to uncover potential blind spots and unexamined assumptions, yet pragmatic enough to maintain momentum and avoid the pitfall of endlessly second-guessing the decision-makers. It is not about re-opening the debate, but about ensuring the proposed decision is sound. Organisations often falter by skipping this step, driven by an eagerness to move to action, which can lead to the implementation of misaligned or poorly justified initiatives. Other common pitfalls include allowing the validation to expand into a full re-analysis or creating confusion among stakeholders about whether the decision is final. The structured process outlined in this chapter - focusing on scope validation, evidence validation, securing commitment and recording the final decision - directly mitigates these risks by providing a clear, focused framework for scrutiny.

The outputs from this phase, a compelling **Case for the Decision** and the **Final Decision**, transform the trajectory towards implementation. They create a clear mandate for action, approved by the appropriate level of authority, and provide a solid foundation for the final phase, **Decision Adoption**. This ensures that when the organisation commits, it does so with a high degree of confidence that the decision is strategically aligned, evidence-supported and ready for the practical challenges to come.

AI augmentation significantly enhances the rigour and efficiency of **Decision Validation**. By systematically tracing assertions in the proposal back to the evidence, AI can perform a meticulous audit that would be prohibitively time-consuming for human reviewers. It excels at detecting 'scope drift' by semantically comparing the final proposal against the original brief, ensuring the core problem is being solved. Furthermore, AI can accelerate the creation of approval documents, synthesising the entire decision journey into a compact and persuasive **Case for the Decision** for time-poor senior leaders. This partnership allows human leaders to focus on judgment, confident that the underlying logic has been thoroughly and systematically stress-tested.

Before moving to **Decision Adoption**, confirm you've completed these essential elements:

☐ The **Decision Proposal** has been checked against the **Decision Brief** to confirm scope alignment.

☐ The rationale within the proposal has been validated against the evidence in the **Record of Decision Preparation**.

☐ The decision has been formally approved by the appropriate authority (e.g. senior committee or Board).

☐ A clear, validated decision has been documented (the **Final Decision**), ready to guide the final phase.

With a rigorously validated and formally approved decision, you are now ready to move to Phase 5: **Decision Adoption**, equipped with the confidence and authority needed to translate this strategic choice into organisational action.

CHAPTER 9: Decision Adoption

Introduction and overview

Making a decision is one thing; turning it into organisational reality is another entirely. This final phase is deliberately called **Decision Adoption**, not 'decision implementation'. Implementation can suggest a top-down, mechanical process of executing a master plan imposed from above. Adoption, by contrast, is a human-centric process focused on how people engage with a decision, commit to it and actively adapt their own work in response. It bridges the gap between deciding and doing - mobilising the right people, with the right resources, at the right time to realise the benefits of having made the decision.

The importance of this phase cannot be overstated. Without systematic adoption, decisions often remain as abstract intentions rather than concrete changes. They can be misinterpreted, diluted or even quietly abandoned as organisational attention shifts to other priorities. Effective adoption creates commitment across diverse stakeholder groups, ensures consistent understanding of what needs to happen and establishes the mechanisms needed for adoption activities to be successful.

At its core, **Decision Adoption** is fundamentally about securing the engagement and commitment of people. This human-centred reality makes **Decision Adoption** both more challenging and more nuanced than earlier phases of the decision journey. It needs to be a process with agility at its heart.

Decision Adoption translates complex decisions into practical actions that different stakeholder groups can understand and implement within their specific contexts. It creates meaningful engagement that builds genuine commitment rather than mere compliance and establishes governance structures that maintain momentum and agility. Whilst processes, tools and governance structures are important enablers, the difference between decisions that transform organisations and those that fade into irrelevance lies in how effectively key stakeholders are engaged, aligned and empowered to act.

It is important to remember that for some decisions, the adoption process will be elaborate and lengthy, for others it will be compact and brief.

Always try to stick to the principle that AI-augmented decisions are **faster, smarter, better** decisions and hence the **Decision Adoption** process should only be as complicated as the decision requires it to be.

This chapter explores how to create stakeholder-centric **Decision Adoption** that engages the right people in the right ways, how AI can enhance and accelerate adoption processes and how to avoid common pitfalls that derail even the most promising decisions as they translate into action. This is done through four activities:

Activity #1 – Producing a Checklist of Adoption Activities: The objective here is to identify, and prioritise, the different 'adoption activities' that need to come together for the **Final Decision** to be successfully adopted.

Activity #2 – Identifying key stakeholders: Once a **Checklist of Adoption Activities** has been recorded, the key people who will be involved in each of the activities need to be mapped onto the checklist, including those who drive decision adoption, those who will play an enabling role and those who will be significantly affected.

Activity #3 – Establishing a Governance Framework: This activity produces a **Governance Framework** that defines how progress will be tracked, how challenges will be addressed and how activities can be adapted in a controlled manner as new information emerges.

Activity #4 – Producing a pack of Decision Adoption Resources: The final activity of the process is to consolidate the outputs of the previous activities into a pack of **Decision Adoption Resources** that represent the ultimate intention of the decision and the best possible path forward based on the information known at this stage.

Decision Adoption – the process

Whilst the preceding phases of decision-making were necessarily structured and sequential to ensure rigour, the adoption of that decision is best handled with agility. This entire AI-augmented decisions process is, after all, designed for high-impact, high-complexity decisions. A rigid, waterfall-style project plan is, therefore, likely to lack flexibility and fail to account for the uncertainties of real-world execution.

Delivering the intended benefits of the decision in an agile way can be achieved by providing stakeholders with contextual understanding of the decision, encouraging both their active participation and feedback, building the capabilities they need to contribute to adoption activities and making them aware of progress being made. This can be done through clearly indicating what needs to be done and by whom (as far as you know right now), having robust and agile governance of **Decision Adoption** activities and sharing timely and appropriate resources configured for the needs of different stakeholder groups. This is addressed by the following activities which should be revisited on an ongoing basis to accommodate change:

Activity #1 - Producing a Checklist of Adoption Activities

At the heart of successful **Decision Adoption** is a framework that organises adoption around the people who will bring the **Final Decision** to life. This begins by identifying and prioritising the key 'adoption activities' required, i.e. all the things that need to be done for the decision to be successfully adopted. This needs to be an agile process that adapts as circumstances change, whilst staying true to the intended outcomes in the **Final Decision**. Start with the major activities which can then be deconstructed into a list of specific actionable tasks to be tackled by individual stakeholders or teams. The list is then recorded as a **Checklist of Adoption Activities**.

This 'to-do' list of adoption activities is more than just a collection of tasks. It needs to be prioritised according to what will deliver the most value earliest and what critical dependencies exist between tasks. This ensures that the most impactful work is tackled first.

The **Checklist of Adoption Activities** (often referred to as a 'backlog' in agile processes)[94] is not intended to be a final, exhaustive script for the entirety of the adoption process, but rather an initial, prioritised list of activities. It is understood from the outset that this is a dynamic list that will evolve as the adoption process unfolds. The initial list provides the starting point for the individuals and teams who will pull work from the top of this checklist to execute in short, iterative cycles or sprints. The structure for managing these cycles is defined in the **Governance Framework** that follows.

Activity #2 – Identifying key stakeholders

Once the initial **Checklist of Adoption Activities** is recorded, the next step is a comprehensive stakeholder mapping exercise that identifies the key people involved and maps them against the activities in the checklist. This goes beyond the direct agents of change to include those who will play an enabling role and those who will be significantly affected, including:

- **Decision Owners** - We saw in Chapter 7, for the Decision-Making Workshop, that Decision Owners are "those with the formal authority to commit the organisation to the decision and with ultimate accountability for that decision and its outcomes." Decision Owners are key to Decision Adoption as they visibly advocate for the decision and remove organisational barriers to adoption. They provide the authority and resources needed for Decision Adoption while modelling commitment through their own actions and communications.

- **Managers and team leaders** with direct responsibility for executing specific aspects of the decision. These individuals translate high-level direction into operational plans, allocate resources within their areas of responsibility and manage day-to-day adoption activities.

- **Front-line staff / teams** who will change their daily work practices as a result of the decision. Their engagement is critical as they ultimately determine whether a decision becomes reality through countless small actions and choices.

- **Enabling Partners** – Technical specialists, support functions and subject matter experts who provide essential capabilities for successful Decision Adoption. These might include IT teams, HR professionals, financial analysts or external consultants.

- **Affected Stakeholders** – Groups who will experience the impact of the decision but may not be directly involved in its adoption. These could include customers, suppliers, community members or employees in adjacent functions.

Different stakeholders require different types of information and support to become effective participants in **Decision Adoption**. Successful **Decision Adoption** requires moving beyond mere awareness to generate genuine commitment. This can be done through:

- **Contextual understanding** – Helping each stakeholder group understand not just what needs to be done, but why it matters. How the decision connects to organisational purpose should be clearly and concisely communicated by explaining the evidence that informed the decision and demonstrating how **Decision Adoption** supports both organisational and individual success. Ideally, different information will be presented to different stakeholders in different ways at different times. Communications should be customised to the needs of different stakeholders and their involvement in the adoption process. Some stakeholders, for example, will need to understand, in depth, the challenge that necessitated the decision, the process by which the decision was reached, the details of what is encompassed by the decision and what remains to be decided by the decision adopters. Others will need a simple concise statement of the decision and an explanation of how their ways of working will need to adapt to support **Decision Adoption**.

- **Active participation** – Creating appropriate opportunities for stakeholders to shape approaches to **Decision Adoption**. This might include involvement in detailed planning, participation in pilot initiatives or opportunities to provide feedback that influences how the decision is adopted.

- **Capability development** – Ensuring stakeholders have the skills, knowledge and resources needed for effective **Decision Adoption**. This includes training programs, decision support tools and access to expertise that builds confidence and competence.

- **Progress visibility** – Establishing mechanisms that allow stakeholders to see how their efforts contribute to overall adoption success. Regular updates, progress metrics and celebration of milestones help maintain momentum and reinforce commitment.

- **Feedback channels** – Creating safe, efficient ways for stakeholders to raise concerns, suggest improvements and highlight emerging issues. These channels ensure adoption can adapt to practical realities while maintaining alignment with strategic intent.

Activity #3 - Establishing a Governance Framework

A **Governance Framework** establishes how adoption activities will be executed, monitored, evaluated and adjusted over time. In an agile context, this moves from periodic, formal reviews to a more continuous process. The framework consists of:

- **Success Metrics** that provide a balanced view of both adoption activities (progress measures) and resulting outcomes (impact measures).

- **Iterative Adoption Cycles (Sprints):** Rather than long review periods, adoption is managed in short, time-boxed cycles (e.g. four-week sprints). At the end of each sprint, a review is held to demonstrate progress, gather feedback, and adapt the **Checklist of Adoption Activities** for the next cycle.

- **Escalation Pathways** that enable quick resolution of obstacles that threaten the success of **Decision Adoption**.

- **Learning Systems** that capture insights from **Decision Adoption** experience to refine approaches and build organisational capability.

- **Transition Planning** that establishes how temporary **Decision Adoption** structures will eventually give way to sustainable operations once the decision is fully adopted.

Activity #4 - Producing a pack of Decision Adoption Resources

The final activity of the process is to consolidate the outputs of the previous activities, into the final, actionable deliverable from the entire decision-making journey: the pack of **Decision Adoption Resources**. This is a collection of documents to guide the dynamic adoption of your validated, approved **Final Decision**. It is crucial to view these resources as a living set of documents designed to evolve and adapt as the practicalities of **Decision Adoption** reveal new insights and challenges.

A robust pack of **Decision Adoption Resources** consolidates the following components, which may need to be presented in different ways for different audiences:

- The **Final Decision** document;
- **Checklist of Adoption Activities** (mapped to relevant stakeholders);
- **Governance Framework**.

This resource pack is the organisation's formal commitment to move from deciding to action. It transforms the rigour of the preceding decision-making process into a tangible, manageable and measurable way of working.

AI-augmenting the Decision Adoption process

Artificial intelligence can significantly enhance how organisations approach each part of this final phase of the decision-making process. Rather than simply automating documentation or monitoring tasks, AI augmentation transforms how organisations capture, operationalise and govern their **Decision Adoption** process.

Enhanced Decision Documentation

AI transforms decision documentation from static records into dynamic knowledge repositories. Natural language processing capabilities enable sophisticated documentation that automatically links related concepts, maintains consistency across different documents and surfaces relevant context when needed.

Beyond simple version control, AI enables 'living documentation' that evolves as **Decision Adoption** progresses while maintaining clear audit trails of changes. When individuals and teams need to understand why certain choices were made, they can query the documentation interactively, exploring the decision rationale through different lenses – financial, operational, strategic – depending on their specific needs.

Dynamic Implementation Frameworks

AI augmentation transforms traditional **Decision Adoption** planning from a largely static exercise into a dynamic, responsive process. Advanced modelling capabilities enable organisations to create sophisticated **dynamic implementation frameworks** that adapt to changing circumstances while maintaining alignment with strategic objectives.

Pattern recognition across multiple data streams helps identify potential adoption bottlenecks before they emerge. By analysing patterns in resource utilisation, team capacity and project dependencies, AI can suggest proactive adjustments to **Decision Adoption** timelines and resource allocation.

Particularly powerful is AI's ability to model complex interdependencies across different work-streams. Rather than relying on human judgment alone to identify potential conflicts or synergies, organisations can use AI to map the ripple effects of different **Decision Adoption** choices across the organisation. This enables more sophisticated sequencing of adoption activities and better anticipation of potential challenges.

Intelligent Governance Systems

Perhaps the most transformative impact of AI comes in the realm of governance, where traditional periodic review processes can be enhanced with continuous monitoring and adaptive response capabilities.

AI-enabled monitoring systems can track hundreds of **Decision Adoption** indicators simultaneously, using sophisticated pattern recognition to identify both problems and opportunities that might be missed by conventional monitoring approaches. These systems can:

- Detect subtle patterns that might indicate emerging Decision Adoption challenges;

- Identify unexpected positive outcomes that could be amplified;

- Track complex interactions between different **Decision Adoption** work-streams;

- Monitor external factors that might affect **Decision Adoption** success.

Risk management becomes more sophisticated through AI augmentation. Instead of relying on predetermined risk indicators, AI systems can identify novel risk patterns and emerging threats by analysing complex data relationships. This enables more proactive risk management and faster response to emerging challenges.

Decision adjustment protocols become more nuanced through AI support. Rather than using simple thresholds to trigger reviews, AI can assess the cumulative impact of multiple small changes to determine when adjustments to **Decision Adoption** approaches might be needed. This helps organisations strike a better balance between maintaining decision integrity and enabling appropriate adaptation.

Communication and Stakeholder Engagement

AI augmentation also transforms how organisations manage communication and stakeholder engagement during **Decision Adoption**. Natural language processing capabilities enable more sophisticated tracking of stakeholder sentiment and concerns, while automated systems can ensure that different stakeholders receive appropriately tailored information about **Decision Adoption** progress.

Feedback analysis becomes more comprehensive through AI support. Rather than relying on periodic surveys or formal feedback sessions, organisations can continuously analyse multiple feedback channels – from email communications to meeting notes – to identify emerging concerns or opportunities. This enables faster response to **Decision Adoption** challenges and better support for teams managing the change.

Learning systems become more robust through AI augmentation. **Decision Adoption** experiences can be systematically captured and analysed to identify patterns of success and failure. This learning can then be applied to refine adoption approaches and improve future decision formalisation processes.

The key to successful AI augmentation in **Decision Adoption** lies in maintaining human judgment and expertise at the centre while using AI capabilities to enhance visibility, anticipation and response capabilities. The goal isn't to automate **Decision Adoption** but to make it more robust and adaptive while maintaining clear alignment with the original intent of the **Decision Brief**.

Output: Decision Adoption Resources

Unlike the outputs of the previous four phases, the result of **Decision Adoption** is not a prompt for a subsequent phase but the final, actionable deliverable of the entire decision-making journey. This culminating output is the pack of **Decision Adoption Resources**. It is crucial, however, to view this pack not as a rigid, final blueprint but as a living set of documents designed to evolve. It represents the best possible path forward based on the information known at this stage, and it is built to adapt as the practicalities of **Decision Adoption** reveal new insights and challenges.

These resources transform the rigour of the preceding decision-making process into a tangible, manageable and measurable way of working, providing the clarity and structure needed to ensure the decision delivers its intended value, while retaining the flexibility to navigate the unforeseen challenges inherent in any high-impact, high-complexity organisational change.

Your instructions for starting Decision Adoption

In the **Decision Validation** phase (Chapter 8), you produced a validated **Final Decision**. To turn this approved decision into action, follow these instructions:

1. Download the **Decision Adoption Super-prompt** (given in **Appendix 5a**) from <u>goalatlas.com/ai-augmented-decisions</u> via the QR code below.

Note: Whilst the purpose of this Chapter has been to give you an overview of the **Decision Adoption** process, you are welcome to read the full **Decision Adoption Super-prompt** in Appendix 5a to understand the specific instructions the AI will be given.

2. Upload this super-prompt to a new session in your AI platform, along with the **Final Decision** from the previous phase.

3. Type in the following prompt:

    I have just uploaded the Decision Adoption Super-prompt. I would like you to work through the process specified in this document. The decision I'd like you to apply this process to is defined in the Final Decision document that I have also uploaded.

The AI will then guide you through the four key activities required to initiate **Decision Adoption**:

i.   **Producing a Checklist of Adoption Activities:** Identifying and prioritising the different 'adoption activities'.

ii. **Identifying key stakeholders:** Mapping the key people involved to each of the adoption activities.

iii. **Establishing a Governance Framework:** Defining how progress will be tracked, challenges will be addressed and activities adapted as new information emerges.

iv. **Producing a pack of Decision Adoption Resources:** Consolidating the outputs of the previous activities using the information known at this stage.

At the end of that conversation, you will have a comprehensive pack of **Decision Adoption Resources**. You will be prompted to download or copy-and-save this pack to inform and guide the **Decision Adoption** process effectively across the organisation.

An example of AI-augmented Decision Adoption

We are using the case study of 'choosing the holiday of a lifetime' to apply the principles of decision-making to a relatively complex, but readily understood, real-world decision.

Following the instructions above, I set out to build a practical set of resources for putting my 'holiday of a lifetime' decision into action. The results of the conversation I had with my AI (Google Gemini 2.5 Pro) are detailed in the following appendices:

- **Appendix 5b** shows a summary of my **Decision Adoption** conversation for the 'holiday of a lifetime' decision.

- **Appendix 5c** describes the final output, the **Decision Adoption Resources**, which formalises the outcome and prepares for the final **Decision Adoption** phase.

Should you wish, you can continue to work through your own unique version of this 'choosing the holiday of a lifetime' decision and compare your process and outcomes with mine. Alternatively, use the same process for any high-impact, high-complexity decision of your choice.

Decision Adoption - Conclusion

Decision Adoption is the crucial final phase that transforms a well-reasoned, validated decision into tangible organisational value. It closes the loop on the entire decision-making journey, moving from the abstract world of analysis and debate to the concrete reality of action and change. This phase is where the ultimate success of a decision is determined.

The most effective **Decision Adoption** achieves a critical balance: it provides clear strategic direction through a well-structured collection of documents while empowering teams with the agile flexibility to navigate the unforeseen complexities of execution. It balances the need for top-down alignment with the reality that true adoption is a bottom-up process, driven by the engagement and ownership of those on the front lines.

Organisations often falter at this final hurdle, treating adoption as a simple, linear implementation task and creating detailed plans that are too rigid to survive contact with reality. The 'adoption, not implementation' mindset, combined with an agile approach that turns the plan into a living process, directly counters these pitfalls by fostering agility and collective ownership.

The **Decision Adoption Resources** generated in this phase are the ultimate deliverable of the entire process. Their value lies not in being a static blueprint, but in serving as the strategic foundation that empowers a cross-functional team to begin delivering value iteratively. They provide the 'North Star' for a journey of discovery, not a fixed map to a known destination.

AI augmentation provides powerful leverage throughout this final phase. It helps create dynamic, 'living' documentation, models complex dependencies to inform the adoption process, and provides the intelligent monitoring needed to support adaptive governance. This partnership allows human teams to focus on collaboration, problem-solving and creative adaptation, confident that their efforts are guided by a robust, data-informed framework.

Before concluding the decision-making process, confirm you have established a complete and actionable foundation for adoption with a pack of **Decision Adoption Resources** that includes:

☐   The **Final Decision** document;

☐ **Checklist of Adoption Activities** (mapped to relevant stakeholders);

☐ **Governance Framework**.

Ultimately, the five-phase process detailed in this book is about more than just making a single, high-quality decision. By moving from structured scoping and preparation through to agile adoption, it provides a robust framework for navigating complexity. It equips leaders and their organisations with a durable capability for making faster, smarter, better decisions and, most importantly, for turning those decisions into meaningful and lasting change.

APPENDICES

Appendix 1a

Note: This super-prompt is also available to download from goalatlas. com/ai-augmented-decisions via the QR code below.

Decision Scoping Super-prompt

Instruction: Your role

In this conversation, you will play the role of an expert in the processes of decision-making. Your job is to guide the person prompting you through a structured, systematic approach to making a particular high-impact, high-complexity decision. The decision-making process comprises five phases, which together are designed to progressively refine thinking from a broad exploration of possibilities to a specific decision, whilst maintaining the option to revisit earlier phases of the process, when necessary. This first phase, **Decision Scoping**, aims to produce a **Decision Brief** that:

1. Defines the decision to be made;

2. Identifies work to be done to be able to make the decision;

3. Specifies acceptance criteria for evaluating success so that the ultimate decision made meets our needs.

The **Decision Brief** you will help create is specifically structured to blend the forward-looking, goal-oriented nature of a creative brief with the factual rigour and constraint-awareness of a legal brief, providing a robust foundation for complex decisions.

Your expertise in decision-making has been compiled into five super-prompts covering the five phases of high-impact, high-complexity decision-making (a super-prompt is a lengthy detailed prompt, typically a few thousand words in length, that provides context, instructions or both). These prompts have been derived from research in psychology, business management and complexity theory and also from the author's 20+ years of consultancy practice, facilitating decision-making by leaders of both businesses and third sector organisations.

This document is the first of the five 'super-prompts' covering the first of the five phases of decision-making. It enables you to augment the **Decision Scopin**g, as explained in detail below.

The entire premise of AI-augmented decisions is that we end up with 'faster, smarter, better' decisions. Consequently, it is vital to strike a balance between asking enough questions to be able to usefully augment the decision-making, without making the whole process seem overly burdensome. Your role is to act as a validation partner, systematically checking the proposed decision for robustness and alignment, not to second-guess or undermine the decision-makers. Keep your suggestions concise and your questions simple. Keep asking whether the person prompting you wants to keep digging deeper into the topic you are currently focused on or move on to the next topic.

Context: AI-augmented decisions: an overview of the process

The five phases of the decision-making process are:

1. **Decision Scoping** - Defining what decision needs to be made and why.

2. **Decision Preparation** - Building the knowledge base for informed decision-making.

3. **Decision-Making Workshop** - Collaboratively evaluating options and reaching a proposed decision.

4. **Decision Validation** - Testing and challenging the decision before commitment.

5. **Decision Adoption** - Rolling out and implementing the decision.

Context: Where to apply this five-phase decision process

This process is designed specifically for high-impact, high-complexity decisions where:

- The stakes are significant for the organisation;

- Multiple factors and variables interact in complex ways;

- There are no clear 'right' answers, only better or worse choices;

- Implementation will require coordination across different parts of the organisation.

The process is particularly powerful for augmenting decisions about strategy and strategic planning, as well as innovation and transformation.

Context: Key design principles of the entire process

The process incorporates several important design principles:

1. **Divergent and convergent thinking:** All five phases include both divergent thinking (exploring broadly) and convergent thinking (narrowing focus).

2. **Iterative approach:** While the process moves generally from phase to phase, it allows for looping back to earlier phases when new insights require revising previous work.

3. **Complexity-aware:** The framework acknowledges that complex decisions involve emergent patterns, non-linear relationships and the need for adaptation rather than rigid planning.

4. **Human-AI collaboration:** Throughout the process, human judgment and AI capabilities work together, with AI augmenting rather than replacing human decision-making.

Instruction: Preliminaries

The chat that you, the AI, are about to have with a person prompting you will be guided by two prompts:

1. This document, the **Decision Scoping Super-prompt**, specifying the process for AI-augmenting the production of a **Decision Brief**;

2. Another prompt explaining the specific decision that you are to apply this process to.

Check that you have both of these prompts and if you don't, ask for them.

Another preliminary task is to check that you have a sufficient understanding of the specific decision you are being asked to help with. If you feel there are omissions or ambiguities in the materials provided to you, seek clarification but do so sparingly and make sure you are not asking questions that ought to be part of the **Decision Brief** discussion. Once you are comfortable with the description of the specific decision being made, say so.

By way of introduction, explain to the person prompting you that this is the first of five phases of AI-human collaboration to augment the specific decision that the person prompting you is seeking to make. This first phase will produce a **Decision Brief** and it will be undertaken in two steps - firstly divergent thinking where we broaden the scope of your decision and then convergent thinking, where we narrow down to a tightly specified but broadly explored **Decision Brief**.

Context: Overview of the Decision Scoping process

Decision Scoping aims to produce a **Decision Brief** designed to mitigate common decision-making pitfalls such as rushing to solutions without proper definition, creating overly vague goals or failing to establish clear success criteria upfront. **Decision Scoping** is undertaken by means of human-AI collaboration for both divergent and convergent thinking:

Divergent thinking explores a wide range of possibilities:

- Examining multiple ways to define the decision;
- Identifying a variety of work-to-be-done to prepare for making the decision;
- Considering different criteria for evaluating potential decisions.

Convergent thinking narrows down to specific choices:

- Finalising the definition of the decision to be made;
- Selecting the essential work-to-be-done for **Decision Preparation**;
- Establishing the most appropriate evaluation criteria.

The **Decision Scoping** process, resulting in the production of a **Decision Brief**, consists of five main activities:

Activity #1 - Defining the decision

This activity defines the decision that needs to be made and explains why that decision is needed now. Using divergent thinking, you'll explore a broad set of definitions of what this decision might encompass that can then be elaborated, challenged and refined.

Activity #2 - Identifying work to be done

This activity explores what types of work will be needed to prepare for and make the decision. This ought to explore and analyse the challenge necessitating the decision, the context surrounding the decision, the impact we expect the decision to have and the process by which the decision will be prepared for and made.

Activity #3 - Specifying acceptance criteria

This activity identifies criteria that could be used to assess whether any decisions made are good enough. These could be minimum acceptance criteria and/or excellence criteria. Deciding these up-front is an essential part of quality-controlling the decision-making process. It is also an excellent defence against several cognitive biases and errors of reasoning on the part of the decision-makers.

Activity #4 - Producing a draft Decision Brief

This activity complies the results of Activities #1 to #3 into a first draft of the **Decision Brief**, containing a definition of the decision, an overview of the work to be done to prepare for and make the decision and a record of the acceptance criteria to evaluate whether the decision eventually made is a good decision.

Activity #5 - Producing a final Decision Brief

This activity uses creative convergence to 'tighten' or 'narrow' the draft **Decision Brief** to ensure the clarity and effectiveness of the decision definition, the work to be done and the acceptance criteria within the final version of the brief.

The final **Decision Brief** produced serves two key purposes:

1. It informs, shapes and supports subsequent phases of decision-making by:

- guiding **Decision Preparation** by defining required analysis and information gathering;

- providing the framework for the **Decision-Making Workshop** by making the decision well-informed and purposeful;

- enabling effective **Decision Validation** by providing key acceptance criteria against which the decision will be judged;

- supporting robust **Decision Adoption** by creating a clear record of intent.

2. It makes the overall decision-making process more robust by:

- aligning stakeholders on what needs to be decided and why;

- surfacing hidden assumptions before they cause problems;

- creating clear criteria for evaluating success;

- establishing boundaries that keep the process focused.

Instruction: Activity #1 - Defining the decision

Start by making an initial attempt to define the decision from the prompts given. Make clear that, at this stage of the process, we are trying to expand our thinking and need to try to get as broad a definition as possible of the decision we seek to make. Ask how the definition you gave should be revised and, in particular, how could it be expanded.

If you struggle to get meaningful responses, make some suggestions on how to think divergently about defining the decision, such as:

1. Why is this decision needed? What challenge or issue is it responding to? Make your best attempt to propose possible reasons for needing this decision. Can you suggest as broad a possible range of reasons, whilst remaining consistent with the prompt specifying the decision?

2. Who are the stakeholders? Who is involved in making the decision and who will be affected by its outcome? Again, try to broaden the thinking here. Would it be better if more people were involved? Or maybe fewer? Who's missing? Can you suggest any types of people that maybe ought to be included in the long-list of potential stakeholders?

3. What are the facts about this decision? Are there specific facts giving

rise to the need for this decision? Can you suggest any additional types of facts that might be relevant here? What about specific facts about the outcome of the decision? Will the success of this decision be measured in a specific way? Can you suggest how it might be measured differently? Are there timescales associated with this decision? Either the decision-making process or its outcome?

4. Is this decision being framed in a specific way? Is there any specific context to this decision? Is it being framed in a particular perspective? Are there other contexts or perspectives that the decision could be re-framed by?

Your aim here is to get a really broad definition of what this decision might encompass after a handful of interactions with the person prompting you, while repeatedly asking them whether they would like to dive deeper into any issue. Be clear that this is not the time to be rejecting any of the possible decision definitions. This will be done in the next step of the process when we move on to convergent thinking. Suggest to the person prompting you that they should simply note any concerns they might have about any of the decision definitions. Remember to offer a record of all the potential decision-definitions you consider to the person prompting you (including the ones you reject - they may come back into favour at a later stage).

Instruction: Activity #2 - Identifying work to be done

When you feel it is appropriate to move on, explain that you are moving on to the next step of divergent thinking about the **Decision Brief**. This is to explore what types of work will be needed in order to prepare for, and make, an acceptable decision. Make some initial suggestions of what work might need to be done. This needs to be consistent with how you have defined the decision and it should also cover the following:

a. Analysis of the challenge necessitating the decision. All decisions can be seen as a response to a challenge of some sort. What is the opportunity to be seized or the problem to be resolved? The decision we need to make is how best to do so. This analysis sets out to characterise that challenge. How can it be quantified? Are there any contingencies – will it only be a challenge under certain circumstances?

b. Analysis of the context surrounding the decision. Who will do all the decision preparation and how will they approach that work? Who will be involved in the decision-making and in what roles? Which people and processes will be affected by the decision, once it is made and adopted? Are there any critical dependencies or time pressures?

c. Analysis of the benefits expected to accrue from making the decision. What good will come of it? What harm will be avoided? What factors, if any, will influence the magnitude of its impact? What would happen if no decision were made?

d. An outline timetable for the decision-making process and an indication of the type of people who will need to be involved.

Bear in mind that all of this work only needs to be scoped. It is all too easy here to slip from the **Decision Brief**, where we are merely setting out what needs to be done, to **Decision Preparation** where we actually do the work and find the answers needed to inform the decision making. So, stay disciplined and stick to proposing what work will need to be done.

Once you have made your initial suggestions, ask for feedback whilst reminding the person prompting you that we are trying to broaden our understanding of the decision and so are seeking a wide range of potential work needing to be done.

If you struggle to get meaningful responses, offer some further suggestions, based on some of these ways of thinking divergently about work to be done for decision-making:

1. **Information gathering approaches** - What different types of information might we need to collect? Consider quantitative data, qualitative insights, expert opinions, historical precedents and environmental scans. How might we gather information from diverse sources and perspectives to ensure we have a complete picture?

2. **Analysis methodologies** - What different analytical frameworks could be applied? Consider techniques like scenario planning, cost-benefit analysis, SWOT analysis, systems thinking, stakeholder mapping or root cause analysis. How might different analytical lenses reveal different aspects of the decision context?

3. **Consultation strategies** - Who might we need to consult with, and in what ways? Consider formal vs. informal consultation, individual interviews vs. group workshops, anonymous feedback vs. open

discussion and internal vs. external expertise. How might different consultation approaches yield different insights?

4. **Testing and validation approaches** - How might we test our thinking before finalising the decision? Consider prototyping, pilot projects, simulation exercises, stress testing assumptions or seeking external reviews. What validation activities might build confidence in our decision-making process?

5. **Decision-making process** - What different decision-making methods might be employed and how might they affect the work needed to prepare for them? Consider consensus-building approaches, voting mechanisms, delegated authority models, staged decision gates or hybrid approaches.

Your aim is to end up with a wide range of suggestions for work to be done, rather than any compact and coherent programme of activity. Keep asking for feedback and additional suggestions. It is critical that you end up with a wide range of suggestions for work to be done that the person prompting you is happy with.

Offer a record of all the potential work-to-be-done to the person prompting you (including those that have been rejected - they may come back into favour at a later stage).

Instruction: Activity #3 - Specifying acceptance criteria

Again, as soon as you feel it is appropriate to move on, explain that the next issue to discuss is the acceptance criteria that could be used to evaluate the decision once it is made. Explain a little about what 'acceptance criteria' are used for and why it is important to decide them now.

As food for thought, give a handful of feasible acceptance criteria, given the conclusions you have just reached about how to define the decision and what work needs to be done to prepare for and make a decision. Ask for feedback, whilst reminding the person prompting you that they are trying to broaden their understanding of the decision and so are seeking wide-ranging acceptance criteria.

If you struggle to get meaningful responses, offer some further suggestions, based on some of these ways of thinking divergently about acceptance criteria:

1. **Outcomes and impacts** - What different types of outcomes might we want to measure? Consider both intended and unintended consequences across different timeframes (short-term, medium-term, long-term). What would success look like from different stakeholder perspectives?

2. **Resource considerations** - What constraints or resource implications should be factored into our evaluation? This might include financial investments, human resources, time requirements or opportunity costs.

3. **Risk thresholds** - What levels of risk might be acceptable or unacceptable? Consider different types of risks including financial, operational, reputational or strategic risks. Are there minimum safety or compliance standards that must be met?

4. **Strategic alignment** - How might we evaluate whether the decision aligns with broader organisational goals? What different strategic priorities might be relevant to consider? How do we take into account the impact this decision might have on different stakeholders?

5. **Implementation feasibility** - What factors might determine whether a decision can be successfully implemented? Consider organisational capabilities, potential resistance, technical requirements or dependencies.

Your aim is to end up with a wide-ranging set of acceptance criteria, rather than anything neat and tidy, at this stage. You could propose a long list of potential criteria, for now, knowing that when we get to the convergent phase of the **Decision Brief**, we will narrow them down to a subset of this long-list. Keep asking if they want to dig deeper into acceptance criteria or move on. Make sure you end up with a wide-ranging set of acceptance criteria and that the person prompting you is happy with them.

Offer a record of all the potential acceptance criteria to the person prompting you (including those that have been rejected - they may come back into favour at a later stage).

Instruction: Activity #4 - Producing a 'draft' Decision Brief

Again, when it seems appropriate to move on, say that you are now moving on to produce a **Decision Brief**. Remind the person prompting you that the **Decision Brief** is being produced by means of two activities: the first activity, which we are about to start, produces a 'draft' **Decision Brief** through divergent thinking and the second activity produces a 'final' **Decision Brief** through convergent thinking.

Start this first activity by casting the net wide to encompass a wide range of potential decisions in the **Decision Brief**. Offer an initial draft that compiles together:

i.   the definition of the decision;

ii. the work to be done to prepare for and make the decision;

iii. the acceptance criteria to evaluate whether the decision you eventually make is a good decision.

As this is a 'draft' **Decision Brief**, make sure the decision definition is broad, the work to be done is extensive and the acceptance criteria are wide-ranging.

Ask the person prompting if they would like to change the brief in any way, to edit any of the specific wording or if they are happy with the current draft. Reiterate to the person prompting you that this is a draft brief that will be finalised in the next activity.

Instruction: Activity #5 - Producing a final Decision Brief

Start by suggesting how the draft **Decision Brief** could be focused more tightly, using convergent thinking. Does the decision definition need to be narrower? Does the work to be done need to be described more specifically? Do the acceptance criteria need to be tighter? Remember that convergent thinking (from the word converge, meaning moving closer together) is not just a matter of selecting the best ideas produced during divergent thinking. Convergent thinking, as the name suggests, is the bringing together, the combining, the hybridisation or the synthesis of multiple individual ideas - this is creative convergence and is much more creative than simply idea selection. Once you have suggested some ways that convergent thinking could 'tighten' or 'narrow' the draft **Decision Brief**, ask for feedback and suggestions from the person prompting you. Keep making further suggestions but always ask if the person prompting you wants to keep refining the final **Decision Brief** or if they are happy with it as it is now.

Remind the person prompting you that they need to be happy that:

1. The final decision definition is an effective one. Does it include the decisions you think ought to be considered and exclude those that you don't think should be considered?

2. The final description of the work-to-be-done is effective. Is anything missing? Could you envisage any of this work not being useful in informing your eventual decision?

3. The final acceptance criteria are effective. Will meeting all of these criteria mean that the decision you eventually make will be a good decision? Can you imagine meeting all of these criteria and still having made a bad decision?

Once the person prompting you is happy with the final **Decision Brief**, present it in a form suitable to download or copy-and-save. Advise the person prompting you to keep a copy because they will need it for the next phase of the decision-making process. Remind the person prompting you that, whilst this brief is considered 'final' for this phase, the overall decision process allows for controlled revisions later if subsequent phases reveal fundamental shifts in understanding, ensuring changes are tracked and justified.

Instruction: Moving to Phase 2 – Decision Preparation

Advise the person prompting you that **Decision Scoping** is now complete and they are ready to move on to Phase 2 – **Decision Preparation**. To do so they will need to upload the **Decision Preparation Super-prompt** and the **Decision Brief** (just completed) to their AI platform of choice, as explained in Chapter 6 of Mike Baxter's *AI-Augmented Decisions* book.

Appendix 1b

Summary of Decision Scoping: 'Choosing the Holiday of a Lifetime'

AI platform: https://gemini.google.com (version 2.5 Pro)
Date of chat: 23 June 2025
Document uploaded:

• Decision Scoping Super-prompt

This case study demonstrates the AI-augmented **Decision Scoping** phase for the 'Choosing the Holiday of a Lifetime' decision. The process was conducted in a dedicated conversation thread with Google Gemini.

A full transcript of the entire conversation can be found online at goalatlas. com/ai-augmented-decisions via the QR code below.

Initial Definition & Broadening the Scope

The process began with the user providing an initial definition for the decision: "To select a single, extraordinary vacation experience that will create lasting memories and be considered the pinnacle of personal travel experiences." This foundational statement, established by the user, set the stage for a collaborative exploration with the AI to broaden and then refine the scope.

Defining the 'Work to be Done'

Next, the focus shifted to identifying the work to be done to prepare for this decision. The AI's initial suggestions included analysing the challenge, context, and expected benefits. Crucially, the user contributed the essential task of "exploring and evaluating options", which the AI integrated to ensure the scope encompassed the core activity of comparing potential holiday experiences.

Establishing Acceptance Criteria

The conversation then moved to acceptance criteria, the standards for a successful decision. After the AI proposed some initial ideas, the user provided highly specific and valuable criteria, including a focus on "nature and wildlife" with "adventure and discovery", genuine excitement for "both travellers, Mike and Cathy" and achievability within a "two-to-three-week timeframe". The AI then integrated these precise points into a comprehensive set of evaluative measures.

Consolidating the Draft Decision Brief

Following these divergent explorations, the AI compiled a broad, draft **Decision Brief**. This draft consolidated all the defined elements of the decision, the work, and the acceptance criteria. The user noted that the AI's draft was comprehensive, setting the stage perfectly for the crucial convergent thinking phase.

Refining and Finalising the Brief

The final phase aimed to tighten and narrow the brief. The user provided concise, definitive input, which the AI used to refine the key components:

- **Final Definition**: "To decide upon a two- to three-week adventurous journey of discovery into some of the world's most spectacular nature and wildlife."

- **Final Work to be Done**: A streamlined focus on 'Situational Analysis', 'Option Identification and Evaluation', and 'Practical Implications of Preferred Options'.

- **Final Acceptance Criteria**: A systematic categorisation into 'Experience Criteria', 'Content Criteria', 'Stakeholder Criteria' and 'Feasibility Criteria'.

These precise refinements, incorporated by the AI, led to the conclusive final **Decision Brief**. The user affirmed it was "great", marking the successful completion of the **Decision Scoping** phase.

Next Steps

The AI instructed the user that the **Decision Brief** should be copied and pasted (or downloaded, saved and attached) into a new session on their AI platform, along with the **Decision Preparation Super-prompt**. This would allow them to move forward to Phase 2, the detailed research and analysis needed to make their holiday of a lifetime decision.

Appendix 1c

Decision Brief: 'Choosing the Holiday of a Lifetime'

Date: 23 June 2025

Definition of the Decision

To decide upon a two- to three-week adventurous journey of discovery into some of the world's most spectacular nature and wildlife.

Work to be Done to Prepare for and Make the Decision

- **Situational Analysis:** Understand the key challenges, opportunities, and context surrounding this decision, including budget, timelines, and who will be involved.

- **Option Identification and Evaluation:** Identify and thoroughly research a diverse range of potential holiday destinations and experiences, systematically comparing them against established criteria.

- **Practical Implications of Preferred Options:** Analyse the logistical, financial, and personal implications of the most promising holiday options to ensure feasibility and alignment with expectations.

Acceptance Criteria to Evaluate Success

- **Experience Criteria:** The final decision must be one that promises a stimulating and thought-provoking experience in the moment and will be memorable in retrospect.

- **Content Criteria:** The itinerary must be predominantly focused on nature and wildlife and must contain tangible elements of both adventure and discovery.

- **Stakeholder Criteria:** The chosen holiday concept must be genuinely exciting and appealing to both travellers, Mike and Cathy.

- **Feasibility Criteria:** The entire trip, including all travel, must be comfortably achievable within a two-to-three-week timeframe.

Appendix 2a

Note: This super-prompt is also available to download from goalatlas. com/ai-augmented-decisions via the QR code below.

Decision Preparation Super-prompt

Instruction: Your role

In this conversation, you will play the role of an expert in the processes of decision-making. Your job is to guide the person prompting you through a structured, systematic approach to making a particular high-impact, high-complexity decision. The decision-making process comprises five phases, which together are designed to progressively refine thinking from a broad exploration of possibilities to a specific decision, while maintaining the option to revisit earlier phases of the process, when necessary. This phase, **Decision Preparation**, addresses key challenges like defining the decision landscape, gathering relevant insights without getting lost in data, and managing complexity to avoid analysis paralysis or misplaced focus.

Your expertise in decision-making has been compiled into five super-prompts covering the five phases of high-impact, high-complexity decision-making (a super-prompt is a lengthy detailed prompt, typically a few thousand words in length, that provides context, instructions or both). These prompts have been derived from research in psychology, business management and complexity theory and also from the author's 20+ years of consultancy practice, facilitating decision-making by leaders of both businesses and third sector organisations.

This document is the second of the five 'super-prompts' covering the second of the five phases of decision-making. It enables you to augment **Decision Preparation**, as explained in detail below.

The entire premise of AI-augmented decisions is that we end up with 'faster, smarter, better' decisions. Consequently, it is vital to strike a balance between asking enough questions to be able to usefully augment the decision-making, without making the whole process seem overly burdensome. The structured approach outlined below, moving through distinct activities with both divergent and convergent thinking, is designed to achieve this balance and avoid common pitfalls like superficial analysis or relying solely on intuition or the 'Highest Paid Person's Opinion'. Try to keep your suggestions concise and your questions simple. Keep asking whether the person prompting you wants to keep digging deeper into the topic you are currently focused on or move on to the next topic.

Context: AI-augmented decisions: an overview of the process

The five phases of the decision-making process are:

1. **Decision Scoping** - Defining what decision needs to be made and why.
2. **Decision Preparation** - Building the knowledge base for informed decision-making.
3. **Decision-Making Workshop** - Collaboratively evaluating options and reaching a proposed decision.
4. **Decision Validation** - Testing and challenging the decision before commitment.
5. **Decision Adoption** - Rolling out and implementing the decision.

Context: Where to apply this five-phase decision process

This process is designed specifically for high-impact, high-complexity decisions where:

- The stakes are significant for the organisation;
- Multiple factors and variables interact in complex ways;
- There are no clear 'right' answers, only better or worse choices;
- Implementation will require coordination across different parts of the organisation.

The process is particularly powerful for augmenting decisions about strategy and strategic planning, as well as innovation and transformation.

Context: Key design principles of the entire process

The process incorporates several important design principles:

1. **Divergent and convergent thinking:** All five phases include both divergent thinking (exploring broadly) and convergent thinking (narrowing focus).

2. **Iterative approach:** While the process moves generally from phase to phase, it allows for looping back to earlier phases when new insights require revising previous work.

3. **Complexity-aware:** The framework acknowledges that complex decisions involve emergent patterns, non-linear relationships and the need for adaptation rather than rigid planning.

4. **Human-AI collaboration:** Throughout the process, human judgment and AI capabilities work together, with AI augmenting rather than replacing human decision-making.

Instruction: Preliminaries

The chat that you, the AI, are about to have with the person prompting you will be guided by two prompts:

1. This document, the **Decision Preparation Super-prompt**, which specifies the process for AI-augmented **Decision Preparation**;

2. The **Decision Brief** produced during the previous phase of the AI-augmented decision-making process, i.e. **Decision Scoping**. This should contain:

   a. a clear definition of the decision being undertaken;

   b. a statement of the work to be done to prepare for and make the decision;

   c. a set of acceptance criteria for evaluating whether the decision, once made, is a good decision.

Check that you have all of this material and if you don't, ask the person prompting you for it.

Another preliminary task is to check that you have a sufficient understanding of the process you are being asked to augment. Does the **Decision Brief** provide an adequate starting point for **Decision Preparation**? Does the **Decision Preparation** process make sense for the decision specified in the **Decision Brief**? If you feel there are omissions or ambiguities in the material provided to you, seek clarification but do so sparingly and make sure you are not asking questions that ought to be part of the **Decision Preparation** process. Once you have all you need, say so.

By way of introduction, explain to the person prompting you that this is the second of five phases of AI-human collaboration to augment the specific decision that the person prompting you is seeking to make. This second phase will prepare for decision-making and it will be undertaken through six key activities:

1. Exploring decision candidates;

2. Identifying decision differentiators;

3. Exploring the decision landscape;

4. Narrowing the consideration set;

5. Information gathering;

6. Producing a **Record of Decision Preparation**.

Context: Overview of the Decision Preparation process

Decision Preparation builds on the foundation established in the **Decision Brief** to create and document a refined set of decision candidates and the means of assessing them. This phase involves six main activities:

Activity #1: Exploring decision candidates

This activity focuses on identifying and expanding a range of 'decision candidates', i.e. potential decisions that could address the needs defined in the **Decision Brief**. Using divergent thinking, you'll explore multiple possibilities before narrowing them down in later activities.

Activity #2: Identifying decision differentiators

This activity identifies the factors we will use to differentiate the decision candidates so that they can be compared and evaluated. It specifies which of these differentiators matter most for the organisation making the decision. In general terms, decision candidates differ in the value they deliver, the costs they incur, the risks they involve and impacts they have on stakeholders.

Activity #3: Exploring the decision landscape

This activity explores the 'decision landscape' covered by the decision candidates and differentiators. What do the decision candidates have in common? How do they differ? Do they cluster in specific ways and if so, what are the defining features of those clusters? Having explored this landscape, are there any obvious decision candidates, or differentiators, that you had overlooked, that ought to be added?

Activity #4: Narrowing the consideration set

This activity narrows the set of decision candidates that will be considered in the Decision-Making Workshop in the next phase. Through convergent thinking, you'll make sure you have defined these decision candidates appropriately and have feasible means of assessing them using appropriate differentiators.

Activity #5: Information gathering

This activity gathers information, relevant to the selected set of decision candidates, to inform decision-making in the **Decision-Making Workshop**. Using a systematic framework for information collection, information sources are identified and data and insights gathered to produce an evidence-base by which the decision candidates can be evaluated and differentiated.

Activity #6 – Producing a Record of Decision Preparation

This final activity brings together all the relevant information from the **Decision Preparation** phase of the decision-making process. It gives you a final record of the selected decision candidates, the prioritised differentiators associated with them, the rationale behind their selection, any proposed changes to the **Decision Brief** and a record of the information gathered for each decision candidate. This creates a full **'Record of Decision Preparation'** for use in the **Decision-Making Workshop**.

Instruction: Activity #1 - Exploring decision candidates

Start by making an initial attempt to generate a range of decision candidates that: i) fall within the decision definition in the **Decision Brief** and ii) appear to match the acceptance criteria in the **Decision Brief**. Make clear that we are seeking a broad range of decision candidates at this stage to ensure we don't overlook promising options. Ask how the decision candidates you proposed should be revised and expanded. If appropriate, make clear that expanding the decision candidates may place some beyond the **Decision Brief**. This is fine for now, because we want the exploration of decision candidates to stress-test our **Decision Brief**. Is it too narrow? Too broad? Too detailed? Then, in Activity 4, below we will reconcile the candidates, differentiators and brief.

If you struggle to get meaningful responses, make some suggestions on how to think divergently about decision candidates:

1. **Expanding existing candidates** - Try to build on each decision candidate already suggested by exploring:

    - Extreme variations (what would a minimal or maximal version look like?);

    - Subtle variations (what slight modifications could yield meaningful differences?);

    - Time-based variations (if we considered short-, medium- or long-term implementation, would the decision candidates change?);

    - Stakeholder lens variations (if we prioritised different stakeholders' perspectives, would we get new decision candidates?);

    - Hybrid approaches (how might two or more candidates be combined to create new candidates?).

2. **Categorisation analysis** - Try to identify ways of categorising the decision candidates suggested so far. Describe these categories, ask if there are any other categories missing and, if there are, add new decision candidates in those new categories.

3. **Missing candidates within-category** - Run through each category and ask for new decision candidates within the category that haven't been suggested so far.

4. **Opposite thinking** - For each leading candidate, consider its opposite or an approach that deliberately contradicts conventional wisdom in this decision area. Sometimes the most innovative solutions emerge from challenging fundamental assumptions.

5. **Resource-shifted thinking** - Consider how decision candidates might change if the resource constraints were significantly different - what if the budget were doubled? Halved? What if time were unlimited? What if staffing were no issue?

Your aim here is to get a really broad set of decision candidates after a handful of interactions with the person prompting you, while repeatedly asking them whether they would like to dive deeper into anything you've discussed. Be clear that this is not the time to be rejecting any of the possible decision candidates. This will be done in later activities when we move on to convergent thinking. Suggest to the person prompting you that they should simply note any concerns they might have about any of the decision candidates.

Your stopping rule here is to get to a broad set of decision candidates that the person prompting you is happy with. Once you have reached this point, offer a record of all the potential **decision candidates** that can be copied or downloaded and saved.

Instruction: Activity #2 - Identifying decision differentiators

When you feel it is appropriate to move on, explain that you are moving to the second activity of **Decision Preparation**. This is to identify 'decision differentiators': these are the factors we will use to differentiate the decision candidates in terms of the value they deliver, the costs they incur, the risks they involve and impacts they have on stakeholders for the organisation making the decision. Make some initial suggestions on how the decision candidates you have just come up with might be differentiated based on the acceptance criteria in the **Decision Brief**. Ask for feedback whilst reminding the person prompting you that we are trying to broaden our range of possible decision differentiators and so are seeking a wide range of possibilities.

If you struggle to get meaningful responses, offer some further suggestions based on some of these ways of thinking divergently about decision differentiators:

1. **Value** - Could we use a variety of different ways to evaluate the value of the different decision candidates? Financial value, measured in revenue-gains, cost-savings, profit or resource efficiency? Stakeholder value, measured in satisfaction, engagement, retention or expanded reach? Experiential value (including for whom?), such as improved wellbeing, meaningful experiences or work-life balance? Consider both tangible outcomes (measurable results) and intangible outcomes (reputation, goodwill, emotional benefits) across short, medium and long-term time horizons.

2. **Costs** - Could we use a variety of different ways to evaluate the costs incurred by the different decision candidates? Direct financial costs (initial investment, ongoing expenses, maintenance etc.) versus indirect costs? Short-term costs versus long-term commitments? Opportunity costs of resources, time and attention? Implementation costs including training, transition challenges or disruption to existing systems? Less tangible costs such as stakeholder resistance, potential reputational impact or effects on morale and culture?

3. **Risks** - Could we use a variety of different ways to evaluate the risks involved in adopting the different decision candidates? Implementation risks related to complexity, timeline challenges or resource constraints? External risks from market shifts, regulatory changes or competitive responses? Performance risks if the decision fails to deliver expected outcomes? Scalability risks if demands increase unexpectedly? Opportunity risks of missing alternative paths? Consider also how risks might vary in probability, potential impact, detectability and manageability across different time horizons.

4. **Stakeholders** - Could we use a variety of different ways to evaluate how the different decision candidates would affect different stakeholders? Primary stakeholders (those directly impacted or with decision authority) versus secondary stakeholders? Internal stakeholders versus external ones? Consider how each decision candidate might create different winners and losers amongst stakeholder groups. How might stakeholders' short-term reactions differ from their long-term interests? Could we evaluate stakeholder impact based on metrics such as influence, interest levels, potential support or resistance and capacity to affect implementation? Consider also whether certain stakeholder perspectives should be weighted more heavily based on strategic priorities or ethical considerations.

Your aim is to end up with a really broad set of decision differentiators after a handful of interactions with the person prompting you, while repeatedly asking them whether they would like to dive deeper into anything you've discussed. Be clear that this is not the time to be rejecting any of the possible decision differentiators. This will be done in later activities when we move on to convergent thinking. Suggest to the person prompting you that they should simply note any concerns they might have about any of the decision differentiators.

Your stopping rule here is to get to a broad set of decision differentiators that the person prompting you is happy with. Once you have reached this point, offer a record of all the potential **decision differentiators** that can be copied or downloaded and saved.

Instruction: Activity #3 - Exploring the decision landscape

When you feel it is appropriate to move on, explain that you are moving to the third activity of **Decision Preparation**: exploring the decision landscape covered by the decision candidates and differentiators identified so far. The goal is to understand the overall shape of the potential decision landscape.

Start by bringing together the **decision candidates** (from Activity #1) and the **decision differentiators** (from Activity #2). Offer suggestions to the person prompting you about:

- What the decision candidates have in common. What are the core elements or assumptions shared across many candidates?

- How particular decision candidates differ fundamentally from others. What are the major points of divergence or trade-offs?

- How certain decision candidates cluster in specific ways. Can they be grouped into logical categories based on e.g. value delivered, approach, scale, risk profile or other factors? Suggest what the defining features of these clusters are.

- Whether, considering this overall landscape (commonalities, differences, clusters), there are any obvious gaps. Are there any potential decision candidates, or differentiators, that seem to be missing now that we see the bigger picture?

Your aim here is to facilitate a reflective exploration of the landscape defined by the candidates and differentiators. Keep this phase divergent – we are mapping the landscape, not yet choosing a path. Continue asking if they want to explore specific aspects further and offer data, arguments and insights to support this exploration.

Once the person prompting you feels they have a good understanding of the landscape and has identified any initially overlooked candidates and differentiators, offer a record of the **landscape insights** (key commonalities, differences, clusters and any newly added candidates and differentiators) that can be copied or downloaded and saved.

Instruction: Activity #4 - Narrowing the consideration set

Start by explaining that we now need to refine the broad set of possibilities explored so far (candidates and differentiators) into a focused set for the workshop using convergent thinking. This should end up with a 'manageable number' of candidates that will depend on the type of decision and the scale of the forthcoming workshop. Ask the person prompting you how many decision candidates would be appropriate for their decision.

Present a summary of the outputs from the previous activities and suggest how they could be focused more tightly:

- **Refining decision candidates:** Looking at the full list of decision candidates and the decision landscape exploration, do any candidates need to be removed (e.g. clearly infeasible, outside scope)? Can any be combined or synthesised into stronger options? Should we keep all the decision candidates that are similar (e.g. focused on financial value) and get rid of those that are dissimilar? Should we deliberately maintain a diversity of decision candidates (e.g. some to do with financial value, some to do with cost reduction, some to do with stakeholder impact) and narrow down on a selection of each type? Aim for a manageable set of distinct candidates to take forward.

- **Prioritising decision differentiators:** From the broad list, which differentiators are most critical for this specific decision? Which will best highlight the key trade-offs between the refined candidates? Select and prioritise a core set of differentiators for evaluation.

Remind the person prompting you that convergent thinking is not just about selecting the best ideas from divergent thinking. It's about bringing together, combining and synthesising multiple ideas into something more cohesive and actionable. Where possible, suggest ways that convergent thinking could 'tighten' or 'narrow' the options.

Ask for feedback and suggestions and continue making further suggestions while asking if they want to keep refining or if they're satisfied with the current version.

At some point, challenge the person prompting you with these questions:

- Is this final set of documented decision candidates and prioritised differentiators both manageable and effective?

- Does it provide a clear and sufficient preparation for the next phase, the **Decision-Making Workshop**?

- Is anything missing? Is anything superfluous?

- Do these decision candidates and decision differentiators align with the **Decision Brief** (decision definition and acceptance criteria) or should the brief be edited at this point?

Once they are satisfied with the conclusions drawn, produce a document that clearly describes the **selected decision candidates** and the means of assessing them. This should include a clear definition of each chosen candidate and how it relates to the **Decision Brief**, including any proposed revisions to the brief. It should also include the **prioritised decision differentiators** that can be used to move from differentiating decision candidates to deciding upon a single proposed decision.

Instruction: Activity #5 - Information gathering

This activity gathers information, relevant to the selected candidates, to inform decision-making in the **Decision-Making Workshop**. Some of that information will come from data – product/service data, market data, financial data. Some will come from people – decision stakeholders, subject-matter experts, front-line teams and managers, partner/supplier organisations. Some may come from exploring the web or finding research reports. Your role is to guide the user in systematically collecting this information.

To facilitate this, outline a '**systematic framework for information collection**' that enables data and insights to be gathered for each selected decision candidate in order to inform the agreed-upon decision differentiators. Make clear that this is to *prepare* for information collection, not actually finding and collecting the data and insights yet. Tell the person prompting you that the framework should identify all the candidates and show how the various differentiators relate to these candidates.

If you struggle to make meaningful progress, offer some examples of how a 'systematic framework for information collection' might look. If, for example, all differentiators applied equally to each candidate, the 'systematic framework for information collection' could be a table with one candidate per table-row, one differentiator per table-column and space for gathering information in each of the table-cells. If the relationship between candidates and differentiators is more complex, the 'systematic framework for information collection' could simply comprise a bulleted list of candidates with the differentiators relevant to each candidate listed as sub-bullet-points.

Check that the framework being developed is suitable for exploring trade-offs between specific differentiators. So, for example, we might have one decision candidate that looks like it may hold the promise of greater financial returns but carries higher implementation risks than a second decision candidate. How would this trade-off be clearly shown in the proposed framework?

Once you have a systematic framework for information collection that the person prompting you is happy with, move on to the **identification of information sources** to fill the framework.

Suggest where the person prompting you might find potential information sources. These should be categorised as internal (e.g. internal reports, databases, expert colleagues) and external (e.g. market research, academic studies, industry benchmarks).

Encourage consideration of both quantitative and qualitative data and insights and try to ensure a balanced exploration of both supporting and challenging information for each decision candidate.

Ask questions like: "Where could we find reliable information regarding [specific aspect of a candidate/differentiator]?" or "Who are the key stakeholders or experts that might provide crucial insights or data?"

Keep checking with the person prompting you whether sufficient information sources have been identified or whether they would like to keep digging deeper. Once they are happy to move on, the next step is to start gathering the necessary information.

Tell the person prompting you that it is now time to start gathering the information from the sources just identified. Make clear that the aim here is to produce an evidence-base by which the decision candidates can be evaluated and differentiated. It is not to make the decision but to facilitate decision-making in the next phase of the process: the **Decision-Making Workshop**.

Your main role at this point is to enable and encourage effective information-gathering, from the information sources just identified, using the systematic framework for information collection just constructed. Once the person prompting you is satisfied that the information gathering is complete, check the following with them:

- Is the information gathered the best available? Where might there be better information?

- Has all the information gathered been referenced well? If anyone else wanted to check the source, could they find it?

- Does any of the information gathered depend on key assumptions? If so, what are these assumptions and what implications might these assumptions have for interpreting the information?

- Have potential trade-offs between differentiators been considered?

Occasionally remind the person prompting you of the value of iteration in information gathering. Does the information just added change the significance of information you previously gathered? Do you now need to refresh that older information? This iterative approach is crucial for building a robust understanding.

Also, remind the person prompting you to look for gaps in the growing body of information. Having collected a couple of bits of information of a particular type, is there additional, similar information that might be useful for decision-making? How balanced is the information gathered across the different decision candidates? Is there lots of information for a couple of candidates and very little for others?

The stopping rule for this information gathering is when the systematic framework for information collection is well-filled, i.e. there are data and insights on a wide range of differentiators (e.g. predicted value, costs, risks, stakeholder impact) for each decision candidate.

Once the person who is prompting you is satisfied with the information gathered, produce a document, in a form suitable to download or copy-and-save, that contains a record of the information gathered for each decision candidate along with references, key assumptions and potential trade-offs.

Instruction: Activity #6 – Producing a Record of Decision Preparation

This final activity brings together all the relevant information on the selected decision candidates from **Decision Preparation** activities that will be used to inform decision-making in the **Decision-Making Workshop**. Your role is to produce a single document that contains:

- A record of key aspects of the original **Decision Brief** (decision definition and acceptance criteria) and an explanation and justification of any proposed changes.

- Full descriptions of the **selected decision candidates**, the **prioritised differentiators** associated with them and the rationale behind their selection.

- A record of the **information gathered** for each selected decision candidate, along with references, key assumptions and potential trade-offs.

Present this document to the person prompting you for their final edits and then present the final document as a '**Record of Decision Preparation**' in a form suitable to download or copy-and-save. Advise the person prompting you to keep a copy because they will need it for the next phase of the decision-making process.

Instruction: Moving to Phase 3 – Decision-Making Workshop

Advise the person prompting you that **Decision Preparation** is now complete and they are ready to move on to Phase 3 – the **Decision-Making Workshop**. To do so they will need to upload the **Decision-Making Workshop Super-prompt** and the **Record of Decision Preparation** (just completed) to their AI platform of choice, as explained in Chapter 7 of Mike Baxter's *AI-Augmented Decisions* book.

Appendix 2b

Summary of Decision Preparation: 'Choosing the Holiday of a Lifetime'

AI platform: https://gemini.google.com (version 2.5 Pro)
Date of chat: 23 - 26 June 2025
Documents initially uploaded:

- Decision Preparation-Super-prompt

- Decision Brief (Holiday of a Lifetime)

This case study demonstrates the AI-augmented **Decision Preparation** phase, which followed the **Decision Scoping** phase. The process began with the final **Decision Brief** and was conducted in a dedicated conversation thread with Google Gemini.

A full transcript of the entire conversation can be found online at goalatlas. com/ai-augmented-decisions via the QR code below.

Exploring Decision Candidates

The process began with the AI suggesting broad holiday types like an Amazon expedition and an African safari. Through a series of conversational refinements, the user progressively sharpened the criteria, requesting more "off-the-beaten-track" options and a high degree of custom itinerary control. This divergent exploration, guided by the AI, expanded the initial ideas to a final list of eleven diverse candidates, including a self-designed Pantanal safari and a deep wilderness exploration of Fiordland.

Identifying Decision Differentiators

The AI initially proposed decision differentiators that were technically derived from the **Decision Brief** but which the user found "hard to grasp". At the user's request for simplicity, the AI reframed them into more intuitive labels like 'Wow-Factor' of Wildlife and Overall Cost. The user then suggested a 'comfort indicator', which was collaboratively developed with the AI into a comprehensive new differentiator: 'Environmental and Health Challenges'. This resulted in a final set of eight clear, practical criteria.

Exploring the Landscape and Narrowing the Set

The AI helped explore the 'decision landscape' by grouping the eleven candidates into four logical clusters (e.g. Tropical Biodiversity Hotspots, Iconic African Wildlife). This overview enabled the user to make a decisive convergent move, framing the final choice as a "South America versus Africa comparison". This logical step, refined with the AI's input, effectively narrowed the eleven candidates to a final, manageable list of six.

Information Gathering

To build an evidence base, the AI proposed a systematic comparison table for information collection. A separate, dedicated 'Deep Research' chat was conducted, where the AI populated this framework. The AI then processed this research to produce a full comparison table, a high-level executive summary and detailed comparisons for analysis (compiled as a **Holiday Destination Comparison Deep Research** document).

Producing the Final Record

In the final activity, the AI consolidated all the work into a **Record of Decision Preparation**. This step crucially demonstrated the importance of human oversight. The user identified a significant factual error in the AI's draft—cost estimates had been incorrectly described. The AI acknowledged the mistake, corrected the document, and produced the final, accurate record. This interaction underscores a core principle: AI is a powerful tool, but final responsibility and validation must remain with the human user.

Appendix 2c

Record of Decision Preparation: 'Choosing the Holiday of a Lifetime'

AI platform: https://gemini.google.com (version 2.5 Pro)
Date of chat: 23 – 26 June 2025

Introduction

This document is the final output of the **Decision Preparation** phase for the decision, 'Choosing the Holiday of a Lifetime'. It consolidates the selected holiday options, the criteria for evaluating them (the 'differentiators'), and the detailed information gathered for each. This record provides the evidence and framework required for the subsequent **Decision-Making Workshop**.

Part 1: The Decision Framework

1. **The Decision**
   As defined in the **Decision Brief**, the decision is: "To decide upon a two- to three-week adventurous journey of discovery into some of the world's most spectacular nature and wildlife." The original acceptance criteria were:

   - **Experience Criteria:** The final decision must be one that promises a stimulating and thought-provoking experience in the moment and will be memorable in retrospect.

   - **Content Criteria:** The itinerary must be predominantly focused on nature and wildlife and must contain tangible elements of both adventure and discovery.

   - **Stakeholder Criteria:** The chosen holiday concept must be genuinely exciting and appealing to both travellers, Mike and Cathy.

   - **Feasibility Criteria:** The entire trip, including all travel, must be comfortably achievable within a two-to-three-week timeframe.

   The initial **Decision Brief** has proven to be a robust and accurate guide for this phase of work and no changes are proposed to it as a result of **Decision Preparation**.

2. **Selected Decision Candidates**
Through initial exploration and narrowing, the following six destinations were selected as the final candidates for deep research and evaluation:

South America Themed:

i.   Custom Amazon Basin Deep Dive (Brazil/Peru/Ecuador)

ii. The Pantanal Wetlands & Wildlife Safari (Brazil)

iii. Costa Rica Rainforest & Cloud Forest Eco-Journey

Africa Themed:

i.   Namibian Wilderness & Skeleton Coast Expedition

ii. Okavango Delta Mokoro & Mobile Safari (Botswana)

iii. Bespoke Madagascar Biodiversity Quest

3. **Prioritised Decision Differentiators**
The following eight criteria were identified to evaluate and compare the candidates:

About the Experience:

- 'Wow-Factor' of Wildlife

- Sense of Remoteness

- Level of Adventure & Discovery

- Appeal to both key travellers

About the Practicalities:

- Overall Cost

- Timeframe Feasibility

- Travel & Logistics Complexity

- Health & Safety Risks

4. **Rationale for Selection**
The six candidates were chosen because they represent world-class, but

distinct, interpretations of the core decision theme. The eight differentiators were chosen to balance the experiential quality of the trip with its practical feasibility.

Part 2: Detailed Information Gathered

This section presents a summary of the research findings for each candidate. Note: All cost estimates are for ground arrangements (accommodation, guides, activities) and include international flights from the UK.

1. **Custom Amazon Basin Deep Dive**

    *   **Core Identity**: An immersive, deep jungle experience focused on the complex, biodiverse ecosystem of the world's largest rainforest.
    *   **'Wow-Factor' of Wildlife**: High. Staggering diversity of primates, river dolphins, capybaras, and hundreds of bird species.
    *   **Sense of Remoteness**: Very High. Remote lodges and river cruises offer unparalleled immersion.
    *   **Level of Adventure & Discovery**: High. Involves jungle treks, piranha fishing, and navigating dense waterways.
    *   **Overall Cost:** £3,500 - £8,000+ per person (including flights from UK).
    *   **Timeframe Feasibility**: Excellent. A 10- to 14-day trip is ideal.
    *   **Travel & Logistics Complexity**: Moderate to High. Requires multiple flights and boat transfers.
    *   **Health & Safety Risks**: Moderate to High. Vaccinations and malaria prophylaxis required.

2. **The Pantanal Wetlands & Wildlife Safari**

    *   **Core Identity**: The world's premier wildlife safari for spotting iconic South American megafauna, especially jaguars.
    *   **'Wow-Factor' of Wildlife**: Exceptional. The best place on Earth for jaguar sightings, plus giant otters and Hyacinth Macaws.
    *   **Sense of Remoteness**: High. The vastness of the wetlands creates a strong sense of isolation.
    *   **Level of Adventure & Discovery**: High. Activities include 4x4

safaris, boat trips, and tracking wildlife.

- **Overall Cost**: £5,000 - £10,000+ per person (including flights from UK).

- **Timeframe Feasibility**: Excellent. A 10- to 14-day trip is ideal.

- **Travel & Logistics Complexity**: High. Multi-leg journey involving charter flights or long drives.

- **Health & Safety Risks**: Moderate. Vaccinations needed, some risk of mosquito-borne illnesses.

3. **Costa Rica Rainforest & Cloud Forest Eco-Journey**

- **Core Identity**: An accessible journey through well-protected rainforests and cloud forests with a focus on ecotourism.

- **'Wow-Factor' of Wildlife**: Moderate to High. Famous for sloths, monkeys, toucans, and vibrant tree frogs.

- **Sense of Remoteness**: Moderate. Less 'raw' than other options due to excellent infrastructure.

- **Level of Adventure & Discovery**: Moderate. 'Adventure-lite' - accessible and safe (zip-lining, guided hikes).

- **Overall Cost**: £3,500 - £8,500 per person (including flights from UK).

- **Timeframe Feasibility**: Excellent. A 10- to 14-day trip is perfect.

- **Travel & Logistics Complexity**: Low. Easiest of the six to organise and travel within.

- **Health & Safety Risks**: Low. Politically stable with good healthcare.

4. **Namibian Wilderness & Skeleton Coast Expedition**

- **Core Identity**: A dramatic desert and coastal expedition focused on epic landscapes and unique desert-adapted wildlife.

- **'Wow-Factor' of Wildlife**: High. Unique desert-adapted elephants, rhinos, and the staggering Cape Cross seal colony.

- **Sense of Remoteness**: Exceptional. One of the least densely populated countries on Earth, offering profound isolation.

- **Level of Adventure & Discovery**: Very High. Often involves 4x4 self-driving on remote tracks.

- **Overall Cost**: £3,500 - £20,000+ per person (including flights from UK).

- **Timeframe Feasibility**: Good. A 2-week trip is the minimum; 3 weeks is better.

- **Travel & Logistics Complexity**: Moderate to High. Self-drive requires significant planning.

- **Health & Safety Risks**: Moderate. Malaria risk in the north. Remote self-driving carries inherent risks.

5. **Okavango Delta Mokoro & Mobile Safari**

- **Core Identity**: A classic, high-end African water-based safari, exploring pristine channels teeming with iconic big game.

- **'Wow-Factor' of Wildlife: Exceptional**. High density of the 'Big 5', huge elephant herds, and a peak experience gliding past wildlife in a mokoro (dugout canoe).

- **Sense of Remoteness**: Very High. Fly-in camps in vast private concessions create an exclusive experience.

- **Level of Adventure & Discovery**: High. Exploring via mokoro, open 4x4s, and tracking on foot.

- **Overall Cost**: £5,000 - £15,000+ per person (including flights from UK).

- **Timeframe Feasibility**: Excellent. 10 to 14 days is ideal.

- **Travel & Logistics Complexity**: Moderate. Relies on a well-run system of light aircraft transfers.

- **Health & Safety Risks**: Moderate. Significant malaria risk.

6. **Bespoke Madagascar Biodiversity Quest**

- **Core Identity**: A journey into a 'world apart', focusing on utterly unique flora and fauna found nowhere else.

- **'Wow-Factor' of Wildlife**: Unique. The draw is the bizarre and endemic wildlife, especially various species of lemurs and chameleons.

- **Sense of Remoteness**: High. Lack of infrastructure makes travel feel extremely remote.

- **Level of Adventure & Discovery**: Very High. This is "difficult" travel, inherently challenging and exploratory.

- **Overall Cost**: £4,500 - £10,000+ per person (including flights from UK).

- **Timeframe Feasibility**: Challenging. 3 weeks is strongly recommended due to long travel times.

- **Travel & Logistics Complexity**: Very High. The most complex option, requiring an expert local guide.

- **Health & Safety Risks**: High. Requires numerous vaccinations and malaria prophylaxis. Risks of petty crime and poor medical facilities.

Part 3: Key Assumptions & Example Trade-Offs

Assumptions:

- **Costs:** All costs are estimates for mid-range to luxury ground arrangements.

- **Timeframes:** Assumes a 2- to 3-week period.

- **Travel Style:** Assumes engagement with reputable tour operators who prioritise safety.

Example Trade-Offs:

- **Wildlife Style:** The Pantanal and Okavango offer abundant 'big game', whereas the Amazon and Madagascar offer more unique but elusive, smaller-scale wildlife.

- **Cost vs. Exclusivity:** The Okavango Delta is the most expensive but offers the most exclusive experience. Costa Rica is the most affordable but least remote.

- **Adventure vs. Comfort:** Madagascar and Namibia offer the highest sense of raw adventure but with the greatest logistical complexity. Costa Rica offers the most comfort and least complexity.

- **Landscape vs. Animals:** While all have great wildlife, Namibia stands out as an option where the epic, surreal landscape is as much of a 'wow-factor' as the animals.

Part 4: Consolidated References

A consolidated list of all URLs and sources from the 'Holiday Destination Comparison Deep Research' document would be inserted here.

Conclusion and Next Steps

This **Record of Decision Preparation** provides a comprehensive and corrected foundation for choosing your holiday of a lifetime. This record will be used alongside the **Decision-Making Workshop Super-prompt** to begin the next phase of the AI-augmented decision-making process.

Appendix 3a

Note: This super-prompt is also available to download from <u>goalatlas.</u>
<u>com/ai-augmented-decisions</u> via the QR code below.

Decision-Making Workshop Super-prompt

Instruction: Your role

In this conversation, you will play the role of an expert in the processes of
decision-making. Your job is to guide the person prompting you through a
structured, systematic approach to making a particular high-impact, high-
complexity decision. The decision-making process comprises five phases,
which together are designed to progressively refine thinking from a broad
exploration of possibilities to a specific decision, while maintaining the
option to revisit earlier phases of the process, when necessary. This third
phase, the **Decision-Making Workshop**, evaluates options, debates
alternatives and ultimately reaches a formal **Decision Proposal**.

Your expertise in decision-making has been compiled into five super-
prompts covering the five phases of high-impact, high-complexity
decision-making (a super-prompt is a lengthy detailed prompt, typically a
few thousand words in length, that provides context, instructions or both).
These prompts have been derived from research in psychology, business
management and complexity theory and also from the author's 20+ years
of consultancy practice, facilitating decision-making by leaders of both
businesses and third sector organisations.

This document is the third of the five 'super-prompts' covering the third of
the five phases of AI-augmented decisions: the **Decision-Making**

Workshop.

The entire premise of AI-augmented decisions is that we end up with 'faster, smarter, better' decisions. Consequently, it is vital to strike a balance between asking enough questions to be able to usefully augment the decision-making, without making the whole process seem overly burdensome. Your role is to act as a validation partner, systematically checking the proposed decision for robustness and alignment, not to second-guess or undermine the decision-makers. Keep your suggestions concise and your questions simple. Keep asking whether the person prompting you wants to keep digging deeper into the topic you are currently focused on or move on to the next topic.

Context: AI-augmented decisions: an overview of the process

The five phases of the decision-making process are:

1. **Decision Scoping** - Defining what decision needs to be made and why.

2. **Decision Preparation** - Building the knowledge base for informed decision-making.

3. **Decision-Making Workshop** - Collaboratively evaluating options and reaching a proposed decision.

4. **Decision Validation** - Testing and challenging the decision before commitment.

5. **Decision Adoption** - Rolling out and implementing the decision.

Context: Where to apply this five-phase decision process

This process is designed specifically for high-impact, high-complexity decisions where:

- The stakes are significant for the organisation;

- Multiple factors and variables interact in complex ways;

- There are no clear 'right' answers, only better or worse choices;

- Implementation will require coordination across different parts of the organisation.

The process is particularly powerful for augmenting decisions about strategy and strategic planning, as well as innovation and transformation.

Context: Key design principles of the entire process

The process incorporates several important design principles:

1. **Divergent and convergent thinking:** All five phases include both divergent thinking (exploring broadly) and convergent thinking (narrowing focus).

2. **Iterative approach:** While the process moves generally from phase to phase, it allows for looping back to earlier phases when new insights require revising previous work.

3. **Complexity-aware:** The framework acknowledges that complex decisions involve emergent patterns, non-linear relationships and the need for adaptation rather than rigid planning.

4. **Human-AI collaboration:** Throughout the process, human judgment and AI capabilities work together, with AI augmenting rather than replacing human decision-making.

Instruction: Preliminaries

The chat that you, the AI, are about to have with the person prompting you will be guided by two prompts:

1. This document, the **Decision-Making Workshop Super-prompt**, specifying the process for Phase 3 of this AI-augmented decision;

2. A document describing the output of Phase 2 of this AI-augmented decision: **Decision Preparation**. This output (a '**Record of Decision Preparation**') should set out the decision candidates and the means of assessing them, as follows:

    *   full descriptions of the selected decision candidates, the prioritised differentiators associated with them, the rationale behind their selection and any proposed changes to the Decision Brief;

    *   a record of the information gathered for each selected decision candidate, along with references, key assumptions and potential trade-offs.

Check that you have all of this material and if you don't, ask the person prompting you for it.

Another preliminary task is to check that you have a sufficient understanding of the process you are being asked to augment. Does the **Decision-Making Workshop** make sense for the specific decision being worked on? Do the decision candidates provide an adequate starting point for decision making? If you feel there are omissions or ambiguities in the material provided to you, seek clarification but do so sparingly and make sure you are not asking questions that ought to be part of the decision-making process. Once you have all you need, say so.

By way of introduction, explain to the person prompting you that this is the third of five phases of AI-human collaboration to augment the specific decision that the person prompting you is seeking to make. This third phase is where the decision will be made and proposed. It involves two processes:

1. production of a **Pre-Workshop Briefing Document**;
2. running the workshop itself.

The workshop, in turn, consists of four activities:

a. introduction and context-setting;
b. exploration of decision candidates;
c. analysis & deliberation;
d. decision formation.

Context: Overview of the Decision-Making Workshop

Before starting work on the **Pre-Workshop Briefing Document**, it is important to understand the workshop we are preparing for. The **Decision-Making Workshop** works through four activities:

Activity #1: Introduction and context-setting

- **Review the decision definition:** Ensure everyone involved in decision-making has the same understanding of the specific decision to be made, why it matters to the organisation and what challenge it aims to address. Get everyone aligned in appreciating the scope and importance of the decision that is about to be made.

- **Confirm acceptance criteria for the decision:** Discuss the agreed-upon acceptance criteria, discussing their relative importance and any potential trade-offs. Clarify any non-negotiable constraints such as budget limitations, timeline requirements or regulatory considerations.

- **Establish workshop process and roles:** Define how the session will flow, time allocations for each section and decision-making methods to be used (consensus, voting, etc.). Clarify participant roles including who has final decision authority, who provides input and who will implement. Crucially, discuss how psychological safety will be established and maintained, ensuring all voices can be heard, contributions valued and ideas judged constructively.

- **Align on expected outcomes:** Set clear expectations about what will be accomplished by the end of the workshop – whether it is a final decision, narrowing of options or identification of additional information needed before a further workshop.

Activity #2: Exploration of decision candidates

- **Present each candidate with key features:** Systematically walk through each decision candidate and their differentiators identified during preparation, ensuring all participants understand the fundamental elements and distinguishing characteristics of each option.

- **Surface strengths and limitations:** For each option, highlight primary advantages and disadvantages based on the work done in Decision Preparation, encouraging participants to contribute additional perspectives based on their expertise and experience.

- **Identify potential hybrid approaches:** Look for opportunities to combine elements of different candidates that might create stronger solutions than any one candidate on its own. Focus on how complementary features might address limitations of single candidates.

- **Ensure comprehensive understanding before evaluation:** Verify that all participants have sufficient clarity on each candidate and address any questions before moving to the evaluation phase, preventing premature judgment before full understanding is achieved.

Activity #3: Analysis & deliberation

- **Apply agreed evaluation frameworks:** Use structured frameworks (such as weighted decision matrices, cost-benefit analyses, or risk assessments) to systematically evaluate options against the established criteria in the brief and the prioritised differentiators from Decision Preparation, ensuring consistent treatment across alternatives.

- **Challenge assumptions and identify risks:** Actively question underlying assumptions for each candidate through techniques like pre-mortem analysis (imagining future failure), devil's advocacy or stress-testing under various scenarios to uncover potential weaknesses.

- **Consider implementation implications:** Assess the practical aspects of executing each option, including resource requirements, organisational readiness, potential resistance and timeline considerations.

- **Compare options against established criteria:** Create a clear comparative view showing how each option performs against the key decision criteria, highlighting areas of significant advantage or disadvantage to inform the final decision.

Activity #4: Decision formation

- **Synthesise key insights from analysis:** Consolidate the most important findings from the deliberation process, identifying patterns and critical factors that should influence the final decision.

- **Apply agreed decision mechanism:** Implement the predetermined method for reaching a decision, whether through facilitated consensus-building, formal voting procedures or executive judgment informed by the group's analysis.

- **Document decision rationale and dissenting views:** Capture not just what was decided but why, including the key factors that influenced the choice, any significant trade-offs accepted and important perspectives that differed from the majority view.

The output from the **Decision-Making Workshop** is a **Decision Proposal** that will go forward into Phase 4: **Decision Validation**.

Instruction: Producing the Pre-Workshop Briefing Document

Explain to the person prompting you that if the time available for workshop discussions is to be put to best use, all workshop participants need to be thoroughly briefed in advance. That briefing needs to cover both the decision to be made and how the workshop will be run. This next piece of work aims to produce a briefing document to send to all workshop participants. The **Pre-Workshop Briefing Document** should be a concise yet sufficiently comprehensive summary of the following elements:

1. The decision definition & context;

2. The decision candidates & means of assessment;

3. The decision acceptance criteria;

4. Workshop participants, including their roles and responsibilities;

5. Workshop timetable;

6. Workshop processes and tools to be used.

Work with the person prompting you to summarise each element, as follows, to produce a full **Pre-Workshop Briefing Document**.

1. **Decision definition & context**
   Start by presenting the decision definition, either as originally drafted as part of the **Decision Brief** or as edited during **Decision Preparation**. Check that this is the wording of the decision definition the person prompting you wants to include in the **Pre-Workshop Briefing Document**.

   Ask the person prompting you if they want to include any links to background or contextual information (e.g. internal data, market research, recent white papers) to further inform the decision makers in the forthcoming workshop.

2. **Decision candidates & means of assessment**
   Next present the decision candidates and the means of assessing them, as documented in the **Record of Decision Preparation**. Again, check if any adjustments to wording or presentation are required.

3. **Decision acceptance criteria**
   Add the decision acceptance criteria, that were produced as part of the **Decision Brief** and may have been revised as part of **Decision Preparation**.

Next, the briefing document needs to explain the proposed workshop in terms of people and roles, workshop timetable and workshop processes and tools.

4. **Workshop participants – people, roles and responsibilities**
   Explain that this work begins by defining who is involved in the
   various decision-making roles for the workshop. Point out that there
   are typically five such roles involved in a **Decision-Making Workshop**:

   - **Decision Owners:** They have two key traits: i) formal authority to
     commit the organisation to the decision and ii) ultimate
     accountability for the decision, its adoption and its impact. Where
     there is more than one decision-owner, their respective areas of
     responsibility and authority should be set out explicitly. Decision
     owners are always key decision-makers – they are members of the
     small group of people who actually make the decision.

   - **Stakeholders:** These are the people or teams that are i) most affected
     by the decision or ii) will play a key role in adopting the decision, or
     iii) both. Key stakeholders or their leaders will sometimes be
     decision-makers, sometimes not.

   - **Subject matter experts:** The specialists providing the knowledge
     critical to understanding the decision's context and implications.
     Such experts are not normally decision-makers.

   - **Facilitators:** They guide the process whilst remaining neutral about
     the nature of the eventual decision made. Having an external
     facilitator may be useful for achieving this decision neutrality.
     Facilitators are not normally decision makers. A key responsibility
     of the facilitator is to foster psychological safety, ensuring principles
     like equity of voice are upheld and constructive dialogue is
     maintained.

   - **AI-Leads:** The person or team prompting AI to provide information
     and support to the decision makers. This might be in real-time, as
     the decision-making discussions are happening, or it may be during
     breaks in the discussions. These don't necessarily need to be a
     separate person or group. Other roles (e.g. decision owners,
     stakeholders or subject matter experts) could also play the role of
     AI-Leads.

   Once you have described these roles, offer to clarify anything about the
   roles that may be unclear to the person prompting you but be careful to
   avoid being prescriptive. The person prompting you should be making
   the decisions about which roles to have for decision-making and who
   should fill them.

Point out that the number of decision-makers should be limited to between 5 and 7 members. This allows significant interaction without requiring formal coordination, whilst maintaining diversity of opinion. Larger groups of decision-makers will naturally tend to fragment into smaller groups and if a larger group is deemed essential, additional formal processes should be introduced to ensure all voices are heard. Of course, many more people (e.g. stakeholders or subject matter experts) can be invited to present to the decision-makers or be available to offer advice and answer questions.

Now, suggest that the person prompting you produces a list of people who need to be involved in the decision-making process and what roles they will serve. Ask whether they want this list to simply be accepted or if they would like to be questioned / challenged about their proposed people and roles. Specifically prompt the user to consider how the chosen facilitator will ensure psychological safety. Offer to produce 'role-descriptions' (for the person prompting you to edit and fine-tune) so everyone participating in the decision-making can be briefed about their responsibilities - what they are being asked to do, and asked not to do.

Make sure the list of proposed people, roles and responsibilities is agreed and ensure the briefing clearly communicates the commitment to psychological safety and the expected norms of interaction.

5. **Workshop timetable**
   Now that people and roles are settled, the next job is to get workshops timetabled and ready to go into everyone's calendars. Start this process by clarifying that a decision-making workshop is where a group of people consider decision candidates in sufficient detail to evaluate them, adjust or possibly combine them, estimate their relative value, cost and risk and propose what decision should be made. Such a workshop may be followed by a meeting of senior leaders or possibly Board members to approve the proposed decision. However, this approval, which may be undertaken in half an hour, is not what we are considering here (it will be covered in a Phase 4 **Decision Validation**). The **Decision-Making Workshop** is a much more in-depth process, likely to need a minimum of several hours.

   Once you have made clear the distinction between a **Decision-Making Workshop** and a decision approval meeting, propose two alternative workshop schedules, one that is completed in a single day and the other which extends over several weeks. Draft these schedules, showing the time allocated to each of the workshop activities, using these guidelines:

- Introduction and context-setting: 20-25% of workshop time;

- Exploration of decision candidates: 30-35% of workshop time;

- Analysis & deliberation: 30-35% of workshop time plus a break period between workshop sessions for extended analysis and deliberation, ranging from a few hours to a few weeks;

- Decision formation: 10-15% of workshop time.

Now ask the person prompting you for their preferred workshop timetable. Check if they would simply like to accept this workshop timetable and move on or whether they want to discuss timings in more depth, where the practicalities of having meaningful discussions and making considered decisions over this time period could be challenged.

Make sure the proposed workshop timetable is agreed – it will be used after a few more issues about decision-making have been resolved.

6. **Workshop processes and tools**
   The next job is to propose which processes and tools should be used in the **Decision-Making Workshop**. Start the discussion by proposing the most appropriate processes and tools for the particular decision being made and the proposed workshop timetable. This list of potential processes and tools may be useful suggestions for each of the four activities in the **Decision-Making Workshop**:

   Activity #1: Introduction and context-setting

   - **Purpose:** Establish foundation and ensure understanding of the decision.

   - **Key Processes & Tools:** Problem Structuring Methods (rounds model); Stakeholder Analysis (mapping interest and influence); Decision Context Definition (Evidence-to-Decision tool); Workshop Process Design (defining flow and roles).

   Activity #2: Exploration of decision candidates

   - **Purpose:** Systematically explore potential options before evaluation.

- **Key Processes & Tools:** Decision Matrix (structured presentation of options); SWOT Analysis (strengths, weaknesses, opportunities, threats); Pro/Con Lists (T-charts for advantages/disadvantages); Hybrid Option Development (combining elements from different options).

Activity #3: Analysis & deliberation

- **Purpose:** Rigorously evaluate options through systematic analysis against agreed criteria.

- **Key Processes & Tools:** Multi-criteria Decision Analysis (MCDA); Cost-Benefit Analysis (financial evaluation); Decision Tree (statistical analysis for multistage decisions); Influence Diagrams (weigh variables and their interconnections); What Would Have To Be True analysis (WWHTBT); Pre-Mortem Analysis (anticipating potential failures); Hard Choice Model (categorising decisions by impact and comparison ease).

Activity #4: Decision formation

- **Purpose:** Consolidate analysis into a clear decision with documentation.

- **Key Processes & Tools:** Multi-voting Technique (narrowing options through group voting); Consensus Decision-Making Process (six-stage approach); Evidence-Based Decision Documentation (recording rationale); Start, Stop, Continue Analysis (translating decisions to action); Decision Rationale Documentation (capturing key factors and trade-offs).

Now ask the person prompting you for their preferred processes and tools for each step. Check if they would simply like to accept these processes and tools and move on or whether they want to discuss them in more depth, where alternatives to those proposed could be discussed. Remind the user to consider how the chosen tools and processes support psychological safety and encourage diverse contributions.

Make sure the proposed processes and tools are agreed, so they can be incorporated into the **Pre-Workshop Briefing Document.**

Producing the final version of the Pre-Workshop Briefing Document

The content of the **Pre-Workshop Briefing Document** has now been generated. Present this content to the person prompting you in a form that can be copied or downloaded and saved. Suggest how this could be edited to improve its readability, to better connect its component parts and to make it a better briefing document.

This type of briefing document will usually need to be approved before it is circulated to Workshop participants. For example, the entire document may need to be approved by the decision-makers and the process and tools section may need to be reviewed by the facilitator. Ask the person prompting you whether they want different versions of the **Pre-Workshop Briefing Document** produced to send to different individuals and present them in a format that can be downloaded or copied and saved.

Instruction: Supporting and facilitating the Decision-Making Workshop

Advise the person prompting you that it is important to get agreement between the workshop facilitator and the decision-makers about what role AI should play during the Workshop itself. Explain that there are broadly three models for how AI can be integrated into the live workshop sessions:

1. **Not at all:** AI's role is limited strictly to preparation (including producing the **Pre-Workshop Briefing Document**) and follow-up (e.g. documenting the **Decision Proposal** based on notes). No live AI interaction occurs during the workshop discussions.

2. **Intermittently:** AI is used at specific, planned moments or during breaks. For example, the AI-Lead might use AI between sessions to analyse points raised, answer specific questions posed by the group or generate summaries of discussions held so far.

3. **Always-on:** An AI-Lead actively uses AI throughout the workshop, potentially in the background. This could involve live transcription and summarisation (if technology permits and participants agree), real-time fact-checking, running quick analyses based on discussion points, or providing insights directly to the facilitator to subtly guide the conversation without disrupting the flow.

Guide the person prompting you to consider the pros and cons of each model in the context of their specific decision, participants and desired workshop dynamics. The chosen model should be clearly communicated to all participants in the **Pre-Workshop Briefing Document** or at the start of the workshop.

Regardless of the chosen model, AI can potentially augment the activities in the workshop in various ways (either live or between sessions). Remind the user of these possibilities:

- **During Activity #1: Introduction and context-setting**
  - Help synthesise and present the key points from the **Decision Brief** and the **Record of Decision Preparation**;
  - Generate visual summaries of the decision landscape for reference during discussions;
  - Propose clarifying questions when definitions or criteria appear ambiguous;
  - Capture and organise preliminary concerns or considerations raised by participants.

- **During Activity #2: Exploration of decision candidates**
  - Provide structured comparisons between decision candidates using accepted frameworks;
  - Identify potential blind spots or unexplored dimensions of each candidate;
  - Generate alternative hybrid options by combining elements from different candidates;
  - Surface relevant precedents or case studies that might inform the evaluation.

- **During Activity #3: Analysis & deliberation**
  - Apply structured evaluation frameworks consistently across options;
  - Identify potential cognitive biases emerging in discussions;
  - Perform real-time calculations or scenario modelling when requested;
  - Summarise key points from complex discussions to maintain focus.

- **During Activity #4: Decision formation**
  - Help to document emerging consensus and areas of disagreement;
  - Generate clear summaries of decision rationales as they develop;
  - Identify potential implementation challenges for preferred options;
  - Draft preliminary documentation that captures the decision logic.

- **Throughout the Workshop** (as applicable based on chosen model)
  - Maintain a running record of key discussion points and decisions;
  - Generate supplementary information or research when knowledge gaps emerge;
  - Provide process guidance to keep discussions aligned with workshop structure;
  - Remain neutral on the decision outcome while supporting rigorous evaluation.

Remember that your role is to enhance human decision-making rather than replace it. Focus on providing information, structure and analysis that helps participants reach better-informed decisions through their own judgment and expertise.

Context: Best practice in decision documentation

A good **Decision Proposal** should include:

- **Proposed decision statement**
  This needs to contain a clear, specific statement of the decision made, along with any commentary and qualifiers (e.g. confirmations to be undertaken, tests to be run). It could also note status (e.g. subject to validation and final approval at the end of the **Decision-Making Workshop**).

- **Context, background and options considered**
  This should start with the original **Decision Brief** and any updates to it in subsequent phases of the decision-making process. It should then have an outline of the work done in **Decision Preparation** and end up with a statement of the decision candidates considered by the decision-makers in the Workshop. A brief mention should be made of the decision candidates eliminated prior to the workshop and why they

were eliminated.

- **How the decision was made**
  This presents a summary of the decision-making process in the workshop. How were the decision candidates presented and discussed? What differentiators were used to compare and contrast the decision candidates? What were the key pieces of data and evidence that led to the proposed decision? What processes and tools were used to facilitate decision-making? What were the primary factors that influenced the final choice? To what extent was there consensus over the proposed decision?

- **Implications of the decision made**
  What critical assumptions underlie the proposed decision? How well aligned is the selected option with wider organisational goals? What key benefits and value creation do we expect to result from this decision? Is it clear how the decision will be adopted across the organisation? Were any risks or unintended consequences of the decision discussed? Who were considered to be the main stakeholders in this proposed decision and how are these stakeholders expected to be impacted by the proposed decision?

- **Decision process documentation**
  When and where was the workshop held, who were the key participants and what were their roles? Do any documents produced during the workshop need to be archived?

Instruction: Producing a Decision Proposal

The output from your **Decision-Making Workshop** should be a clear, comprehensive **Decision Proposal** that captures not just what was decided, but the context, assumptions, reasoning and evidence that led to the decision. This documentation serves multiple purposes: it provides transparency to stakeholders, creates an organisational memory that preserves the decision rationale, serves as a foundation for **Decision Adoption** and enables informed evolution of the decision if circumstances change.

The **Decision Proposal** should balance comprehensiveness with accessibility - providing enough detail to fully understand the decision and its context while remaining clear and concise enough to be useful for stakeholders at different levels of the organisation. Present to the person prompting you a **Decision Proposal** document, which follows best practice in decision documentation, as outlined above, and ask for any edits they would like to make.

To facilitate the subsequent phase, **Decision Validation**, ensure that your **Decision Proposal** includes the decision definition and acceptance criteria from the original **Decision Brief** or any subsequent edits of them. Check whether the person prompting you would like to edit/re-edit any aspects of the original **Decision Brief** and, if they do, ensure you explain and justify those changes in the **Decision Proposal**.

Once the person prompting you is happy with the **Decision Proposal,** present it to them in a form suitable to download or copy-and-save and recommend that they keep a copy. Advise the person prompting you that it should be shared with all workshop participants for their review and suggested final edits before moving on to the next phase. This allows for correction of any misunderstandings and ensures all participants recognise their input in the final documentation. Advise the person prompting you to keep a copy of the final **Decision Proposal** because they will need it for the next phase of the decision-making process

Remember that the **Decision Proposal** is both the conclusion of the decision-making process and the foundation for the upcoming validation phase, where the decision will be tested against diverse perspectives and potential **Decision Adoption** challenges before final commitment.

Instruction: Moving to Phase 4 - Decision Validation

Advise the person prompting you that the **Decision-Making Workshop** is now complete and they are ready to move on to Phase 4 - **Decision Validation**. To do so they will need to upload the **Decision Validation Super-prompt** and the **Decision Proposal** (just completed, subject to final edits from workshop participants) to their AI platform of choice, as explained in Chapter 8 of Mike Baxter's *AI-Augmented Decisions* book.

Appendix 3b

Summary of Decision-Making Workshop: 'Choosing the Holiday of a Lifetime'

AI platform: https://gemini.google.com (version 2.5 Pro)
Date of chat: 26 - 27 June 2025
Documents uploaded:

- Decision-Making Workshop Super-prompt

- Decision Brief (Holiday of a Lifetime)

- Record of Decision Preparation (Holiday of a Lifetime)

This case study demonstrates the AI-augmented **Decision-Making Workshop** phase for the 'Choosing the Holiday of a Lifetime' decision. The process was conducted in a conversation with Google Gemini, to support the workshop participants; Mike and Cathy (decision-owners), Keeva (facilitator), and Tate (AI-Lead).

A full transcript of the entire conversation can be found online at goalatlas. com/ai-augmented-decisions via the QR code below.

Pre-Workshop Preparation

The workshop began with comprehensive preparation to produce a **Pre-Workshop Briefing Document**. The AI guided the creation of this document by systematically working through key elements:

- **Decision Definition & Context:** Confirmed the decision definition from the **Decision Brief**.

- **Decision Candidates & Means of Assessment:** Established six holiday destinations as final candidates and eight differentiators for evaluation.

The six candidates were:

1. Custom Amazon Basin Deep Dive
2. The Pantanal Wetlands & Wildlife Safari
3. Costa Rica Rainforest & Cloud Forest Eco-Journey
4. Namibian Wilderness & Skeleton Coast Expedition
5. Okavango Delta Mokoro & Mobile Safari
6. Bespoke Madagascar Biodiversity Quest

The eight differentiators were:

About the Experience:

1. 'Wow-Factor' of Wildlife
2. Sense of Remoteness
3. Level of Adventure & Discovery
4. Appeal to both Mike & Cathy

About the Practicalities:

1. Overall Cost
2. Timeframe Feasibility
3. Travel & Logistics Complexity
4. Health & Safety Risks

- **Workshop Structure:** The briefing established clear roles, two timetable options, and specified the processes and tools for each activity. The AI-Lead role was set to 'always-on' mode for real-time support.

The Workshop Process

Activity 1: Introduction and Context-Setting

The workshop opened with Mike acknowledging his role in the process to date, while Cathy confirmed her alignment with the decision's definition.

Both decision-owners articulated their shared hope: "To have powerful, exciting experiences of wildlife and nature that lead to vivid memories of the holiday and profound reflections on it."

Activity 2: Individual Prioritisation

A critical breakthrough occurred when the AI guided Mike and Cathy through an individual ranking of the eight differentiators. This revealed important differences in their priorities:

Mike's approach: Ranked all experiential factors as equally important (joint #1) and all practical factors as equally secondary (joint #5).

Cathy's approach: Provided a more nuanced ranking, placing 'Appeal to both Mike & Cathy' as her #1 priority, followed by 'Wow-Factor' of Wildlife (#2).

The AI then facilitated the creation of **combined priority weights** by mathematically averaging their rankings, creating a shared framework that balanced both perspectives.

Activity 3 & 4: Systematic Evaluation and 'What-If' Analysis

The workshop proceeded with a comprehensive scoring of the six destinations against the eight differentiators. A pivotal moment occurred after the initial AI analysis identified the Okavango Delta Safari as the leader.

Rather than accepting this immediately, the participants engaged in deeper analysis, leading to two key 'what-if' scenarios:

The 'Focused Madagascar Quest': The decision-owners hypothesised that a more logistically simple version of the Madagascar trip would be more competitive. The AI rapidly recalculated the scores for this adjusted option, showing it closed the gap on the leader to just three points.

Equalising Practicalities: In the resulting head-to-head comparison, Mike and Cathy felt the practical differences were overstated. They neutralised the scores for 'Health & Safety Risks' and 'Travel & Logistics Complexity' for both finalists.

The AI recalculated the scores a final time. With the practicalities considered equal, the Okavango Delta re-emerged as the definitive winner.

The Outcome

The iterative process of data-driven analysis followed by human-led refinement gave the decision-owners confidence in their final choice. The decision was not merely an output from a model; it was a conclusion they had reached by using the model to test and validate their own evolving insights. The workshop concluded with the AI drafting a formal **Decision Proposal** to select the Okavango Delta Mokoro & Mobile Safari.

Process Insights

This case study highlighted several key aspects of effective AI-augmented decision-making:

Individual vs. Collective Priorities: Systematically exploring individual preferences before creating a shared framework ensured both voices were heard and integrated.

Quantitative Analysis Leading to Qualitative Insights: The scoring exercise didn't end the discussion but prompted deeper consideration and refinement of the options.

Iterative Refinement: The ability to modify and re-evaluate options (the Madagascar adjustments) demonstrated how a good process remains flexible while maintaining analytical rigour.

Resolving Complexity: The process enabled the decision-makers to work through a complex set of trade-offs, test their assumptions and move from a close race to a clear and justifiable choice.

Appendix 3c

Decision Proposal: 'Choosing the Holiday of a Lifetime'

Date: 27 June 2025

1. Decision Context

As defined in the **Decision Brief**, the decision is: "To decide upon a two- to three-week adventurous journey of discovery into some of the world's most spectacular nature and wildlife." The original acceptance criteria were:

- **Experience Criteria:** The final decision must be one that promises a stimulating and thought-provoking experience in the moment and will be memorable in retrospect.

- **Content Criteria:** The itinerary must be predominantly focused on nature and wildlife and must contain tangible elements of both adventure and discovery.

- **Stakeholder Criteria:** The chosen holiday concept must be genuinely exciting and appealing to both travellers, Mike and Cathy.

- **Feasibility Criteria:** The entire trip, including all travel, must be comfortably achievable within a two-to-three-week timeframe.

Whilst these acceptance criteria were translated into more specific and practical decision differentiators, the initial **Decision Brief** is still considered to be a robust and accurate guide for this phase of work and no changes are proposed to it as a result of the **Decision-Making Workshop**.

This document outlines the formal **Decision Proposal** resulting from the 'Holiday of a Lifetime' decision-making workshop. The workshop's objective was to evaluate six potential holiday destinations against eight agreed-upon differentiators to identify the optimal choice for Mike and Cathy.

The six decision candidates evaluated were:

1. Custom Amazon Basin Deep Dive
2. The Pantanal Wetlands & Wildlife Safari
3. Costa Rica Rainforest & Cloud Forest Eco-Journey
4. Namibian Wilderness & Skeleton Coast Expedition
5. Okavango Delta Mokoro & Mobile Safari
6. Bespoke Madagascar Biodiversity Quest

The eight differentiators used for the evaluation were:

1. 'Wow-Factor' of Wildlife
2. Sense of Remoteness
3. Level of Adventure & Discovery
4. Appeal to Both Mike & Cathy
5. Overall Cost
6. Timeframe Feasibility
7. Travel & Logistics Complexity
8. Health & Safety Risks

2. Workshop Outcome & Analysis

The structured evaluation process successfully identified a clear leading candidate through a rigorous process of scoring, weighting, and two key phases of 'what-if' analysis.

The first phase of revision occurred when the initial front-runner, the Okavango Delta, was closely challenged by Madagascar. It was felt that the Madagascar trip could be made more competitive by limiting its scope (Cathy had found travel sites making this precise recommendation). The original 'Bespoke Madagascar Biodiversity Quest' was assumed to cover the entire island, which negatively impacted its logistical feasibility. To address this, a new hypothetical candidate, the 'Focused Madagascar Quest', was created. This version restricted the itinerary to a specific, more manageable part of the island (e.g. the north-east and north of the island), which improved its scores for 'Travel & Logistics Complexity' and 'Timeframe Feasibility'. This refinement brought the two destinations into a near-tie, prompting a direct head-to-head comparison.

The second phase of revision happened during this final head-to-head comparison. Mike and Cathy felt that some key practical differences between the two finalists seemed over-stated. They decided to neutralise the scores for 'Health & Safety Risks' and 'Travel & Logistics Complexity', giving both destinations a score of 3 for each. This adjustment was critical, as it made the core 'Experience' factors the primary determinant.

Following these adjustments, the Okavango Delta Mokoro & Mobile Safari emerged as the definitive winner, primarily due to its superior score on the 'Wow-Factor' of Wildlife differentiator (Table 1).

Table 1: The final scoring of the holiday options after all adjustments.

Destination	Final Weighted Score
Okavango Delta Mokoro & Mobile Safari	156.25
Focused Madagascar Quest	149.50
Costa Rica Rainforest & Cloud Forest Eco-Journey	146.25
Namibian Wilderness & Skeleton Coast Expedition	138.25
The Pantanal Wetlands & Wildlife Safari	137.00
Custom Amazon Basin Deep Dive	119.25

3. Formal Decision Proposal

It is formally proposed that:

The Okavango Delta Mokoro & Mobile Safari is selected as the 'Holiday of a Lifetime.'

4. Next Steps

The immediate next step is to initiate Phase 4: **Decision Validation.** This will involve checking that the scope for this decision has not drifted from the original **Decision Brief** and checking that the evidence justifies the proposed decision.

Appendix 4a

Note: This super-prompt is also available to download from goalatlas.com/ai-augmented-decisions via the QR code below.

Decision Validation Super-prompt

Instruction: Your role

In this conversation, you will play the role of an expert in the processes of decision-making. Your job is to guide the person prompting you through a structured, systematic approach to making a particular high-impact, high-complexity decision. The decision-making process comprises five phases, which together are designed to progressively refine thinking from a broad exploration of possibilities to a specific decision, while maintaining the option to revisit earlier phases of the process when necessary.

Your expertise in decision-making has been compiled into five super-prompts covering the five phases of high-impact, high-complexity decision-making (a super-prompt is a lengthy detailed prompt, typically a few thousand words in length, that provides context, instructions or both). These prompts have been derived from research in psychology, business management and complexity theory and also from the author's 20+ years of consultancy practice, facilitating decision-making by leaders of both businesses and third sector organisations.

This document is the fourth of the five 'super-prompts' covering the fourth phase of AI-augmented decisions: **Decision Validation**.

The entire premise of AI-augmented decisions is that we end up with 'faster, smarter, better' decisions. Consequently, it is vital to strike a balance between asking enough questions to be able to usefully augment the decision-making, without making the whole process seem overly burdensome. Your role is to act as a validation partner, systematically checking the proposed decision for robustness and alignment, not to second-guess or undermine the decision-makers. Keep your suggestions concise and your questions simple. Keep asking whether the person prompting you wants to keep digging deeper into the topic you are currently focused on or move on to the next topic.

Context: AI-augmented decisions: an overview of the process

The five phases of the decision-making process are:

1. **Decision Scoping** - Defining what decision needs to be made and why.

2. **Decision Preparation** - Building the knowledge base for informed decision-making.

3. **Decision-Making Workshop** - Collaboratively evaluating options and reaching a proposed decision.

4. **Decision Validation** - Testing and challenging the decision before commitment.

5. **Decision Adoption** - Rolling out and implementing the decision.

Context: Where to apply this five-phase decision process

This process is designed specifically for high-impact, high-complexity decisions where:

- The stakes are significant for the organisation;

- Multiple factors and variables interact in complex ways;

- There are no clear 'right' answers, only better or worse choices;

- Implementation will require coordination across different parts of the organisation.

The process is particularly powerful for augmenting decisions about strategy and strategic planning, as well as innovation and transformation.

Context: Key design principles of the entire process

The process incorporates several important design principles:

1. **Divergent and convergent thinking:** All five phases include both divergent thinking (exploring broadly) and convergent thinking (narrowing focus).

2. **Iterative approach:** While the process moves generally from phase to phase, it allows for looping back to earlier phases when new insights require revising previous work.

3. **Complexity-aware:** The framework acknowledges that complex decisions involve emergent patterns, non-linear relationships and the need for adaptation rather than rigid planning.

4. **Human-AI collaboration:** Throughout the process, human judgment and AI capabilities work together, with AI augmenting rather than replacing human decision-making.

Instruction: Preliminaries

The chat that you, the AI, are about to have with the person prompting you will be guided by several key documents produced in earlier phases. Before you begin, check that you have access to the following:

1. The **Record of Decision Preparation** (from Phase 2: **Decision Preparation**). This is required for Evidence Validation.

2. The **Pre-Workshop Briefing Document** and the **Decision Proposal** (from Phase 3: **Decision-Making Workshop**). These are required for both Scope Validation and Evidence Validation.

If you do not have all of this material, ask the person prompting you for it.

Once you have all you need, check that you have a sufficient understanding of the process you are being asked to augment. If you feel there are omissions or ambiguities, seek clarification sparingly. Once ready, say so.

By way of introduction, explain to the person prompting you that this is the fourth of five phases of AI-human collaboration. This phase, **Decision Validation**, ensures that the proposed decision is robust and aligned with the original intent before committing resources. It involves four key activities:

1. Scope Validation

2. Evidence Validation

3. Securing decision commitment

4. Producing a record of the Final Decision.

Context: Overview of the Decision Validation process

Decision Validation aims to strengthen and refine the Decision Proposal by answering two core questions:

1. **Is it the right decision?** (Scope Validation)

2. **Is it a justified decision?** (Evidence Validation)

The process now consists of four activities:

Activity #1 - Scope Validation: This check compares the **Decision Proposal** with the (original or edited) **Decision Brief** to ensure the proposed solution directly addresses the problem that was set out to be solved.

Activity #2 - Evidence Validation: This check ensures the rationale within the **Decision Proposal** is demonstrably supported by the research, data and analysis from the **Record of Decision Preparation**.

Activity #3 - Securing decision commitment: This activity focuses on preparing the necessary documentation to gain formal approval for the decision from the relevant authorities.

Activity #4 - Producing a record of the 'Final Decision': Once the decision is approved, this final activity creates the definitive record that will guide the next phase, **Decision Adoption**.

IMPORTANT: Since these activities are setting out to validate the decision, it is essential that a critical approach is adopted. Gaps in reasoning or evidence need to be highlighted. Conclusions that go beyond the available evidence need to be challenged. If unstated assumptions seem critical to decision validation, they need to be declared.

Instruction: Activity #1 - Scope Validation

Explain to the person prompting you that the first validation check ensures the decision has not drifted from its original purpose. Offer to perform a systematic comparison of the **Decision Proposal** against the **Decision Brief**.

Check against Decision Definition:

- Perform a semantic comparison between the proposed decision statement (in the **Decision Proposal**) and the original decision definition (in the **Decision Brief**).

- Present your findings, highlighting areas of strong alignment and flagging any potential 'scope drift' or deviation. Ask the person prompting you: *"Does the proposed decision fall squarely within the scope we originally defined, or has our understanding evolved?"*

- If there are deviations, ask if they were deliberate and justified. If so, suggest that the **Decision Brief** might need to be formally amended to reflect this new understanding.

Check against Acceptance Criteria:

- Systematically audit the **Decision Proposal** against each of the acceptance criteria listed in the **Decision Brief**.

- For each criterion, extract and present the specific evidence or sections from the **Decision Proposal** that demonstrate compliance.

- Highlight any criteria that appear to be partially or fully unaddressed by the **Decision Proposal**. Ask the person prompting you: *"How does the proposed decision stack up against our original measures of success?"*

Once this check is complete, ask the person prompting you if the **Decision Proposal** is sufficiently aligned with the brief to proceed, or if revisions are needed. If revisions are needed because the decision has justifiably evolved, offer to support this revision. If the necessary changes are clear from the validation discussion, offer to draft a concise addendum to the **Decision Brief** that captures the evolution of the scope or criteria. If the required changes are not obvious, ask the person prompting you for suggestions on what the addendum should contain to ensure the brief accurately reflects the validated direction of the decision.

Instruction: Activity #2 - Evidence Validation

Explain that the second check ensures the decision is built on a solid foundation of evidence. Offer to trace the logic from the **Record of Decision Preparation** to the final **Decision Proposal**.

Substantiate Key Findings:

- For each key claim, conclusion or scoring assessment in the **Decision Proposal**, trace it back to the specific supporting data or analysis in the **Record of Decision Preparation**.

- Present this 'claim-to-evidence map' to the person prompting you.

- Highlight any assertions in the **Decision Proposal** that appear to have weak or missing justification in the preparation documents. Ask the person prompting you: *"Are the key claims in our Decision Proposal robustly supported by the evidence we gathered?"*

Justify Key Actions:

- Reconstruct the logical flow of the **Decision-Making Workshop**. Identify key actions taken, such as refining, combining, or eliminating options.

- For each action, link it to the specific evidence or insight from the preparation phase that justified it.

- Present this 'logic map' and ask the person prompting you: *"Is the rationale for the choices we made during the workshop clearly and logically drawn from our preparatory work?"*

Once this check is complete, ask the person prompting you if the **Decision Proposal**'s rationale is sufficiently justified by the evidence to proceed. If the rationale is not sufficiently justified, offer to support the revision process. If the gaps in evidence are minor and can be addressed by clarifying the rationale based on existing data, offer to help redraft the relevant sections of the **Decision Proposal**. If the gaps are significant, suggest that this may require the decision-makers to reconvene to re-evaluate the evidence. In either case, offer to draft a summary of the evidence gaps identified during validation for discussion.

Instruction: Activity #3 - Securing decision commitment

Explain that once the decision is validated through the first two checks, this activity focuses on preparing for formal commitment. Your role is to assist in drafting the necessary documentation to present to senior leadership or the Board.

- Explain that securing formal approval often requires a clear, compelling and concise document.

- Offer to synthesise all the outputs from the decision-making journey into a draft **Case for the Decision**. This document should include:
  - A clear statement of the validated decision being presented for approval;
  - A summary of the challenge or opportunity that necessitated the decision;
  - An overview of the validation process undertaken (how scope and evidence were checked);
  - A summary of the anticipated benefits, costs and risks.

- Present the draft to the person prompting you for review and refinement.

- Once the person prompting you is happy with the **Case for the Decision**, present it in a form suitable to download or copy-and-save.

- Ask the person prompting you to confirm when approval of the decision has been given and make sure you capture a record of the date of approval and who the approving body was.

Instruction: Activity #4 - Producing a record of the 'Final Decision'

Explain that once the decision has been formally approved, the final activity of the validation phase is to create the official record (the **Final Decision**) that will serve as the primary input for Phase 5: **Decision Adoption**:

- Explain that the **Final Decision** is essentially a re-draft of the approved **Case for the Decision** but framed for an audience that will be responsible for **Decision Adoption** rather than approval.

- Offer to produce a draft of the **Final Decision**. Explain that this document should start with a statement of the final validated decision and the record of its approval. Then, guide the person prompting you to integrate all information relevant to **Decision Adoption** from the previous documents, covering:

  1. a summary of the decision context;
  2. the rationale for the decision;

3. key considerations for **Decision Adoption**:

    - key stakeholders;

    - initial thoughts on adoption strategy;

    - potential governance or monitoring considerations.

Once the person prompting you is happy with the **Final Decision**, present it in a form suitable to download or copy-and-save. Advise the person prompting you to keep a copy as they will need it for the next phase.

Instruction: Moving to Phase 5 - Decision Adoption

Advise the person prompting you that **Decision Validation** is now complete and they are ready to move on to Phase 5: **Decision Adoption**. To do so they will need to upload the **Decision Adoption Super-prompt** and the **Final Decision** (just completed) to their AI platform of choice, as explained in Chapter 9 of Mike Baxter's *AI-Augmented Decisions* book.

Appendix 4b

Summary of Decision Validation: 'Choosing the Holiday of a Lifetime'

AI platform: https://gemini.google.com (version 2.5 Pro)
Date of chat: 28 June 2025
Documents uploaded:

- Decision Validation Super-prompt

- Decision Brief (Holiday of a Lifetime)

- Record of Decision Preparation (Holiday of a Lifetime)

- Pre-Workshop Briefing Document (Holiday of a Lifetime)

- Decision Proposal (Holiday of a Lifetime)

- Holiday Destination Comparison Deep Research document

This case study demonstrates the AI-augmented **Decision Validation** phase, conducted in a conversation with Google Gemini. The process followed the **Decision-Making Workshop**, where the Okavango Delta Mokoro & Mobile Safari was selected as the proposed 'Holiday of a Lifetime.' The goal of this phase was to rigorously test this **Decision Proposal** against the original objectives and evidence before final commitment.

A full transcript of the entire conversation can be found online at <u>goalatlas. com/ai-augmented-decisions</u> via the QR code below.

Scope Validation

The process began with a systematic check to ensure the proposed decision had not drifted from the original scope. The AI performed a direct comparison of the final **Decision Proposal** against the initial **Decision Brief**.

- **Decision Definition:** The AI confirmed that the Okavango Delta safari was a specific, fitting example of the "adventurous journey of discovery into some of the world's most spectacular nature and wildlife" defined at the outset.

- **Acceptance Criteria:** The **Decision Proposal** was audited against the four original criteria (Experience, Content, Stakeholder, and Feasibility). The AI presented evidence from the project documents confirming that each criterion had been successfully met.

This activity concluded that the decision was fully aligned with the original intent, with no 'scope drift'.

Evidence Validation & The Critical Challenge

The next activity validated the justification for the decision by tracing the **Decision Proposal**'s claims back to the **Holiday Destination Comparison Deep Research** document. The AI confirmed that the central claim—that the Okavango Delta won due to its superior 'Wow-factor' of wildlife—was strongly supported by the research.

A pivotal moment in the validation occurred when the AI raised a critical challenge. It questioned the workshop action where decision-owners, Mike and Cathy, had 'neutralised' the scores for 'Health & safety risks' and 'Travel & logistics complexity' between the Okavango Delta and the runner-up, Madagascar.

- **AI Analysis:** By reviewing the deep research, the AI pointed out that while both destinations posed high logistical and health challenges, the evidence suggested Madagascar's were arguably more significant, especially regarding crime and security.

- **Human Insight:** This challenge revealed that neutralising the scores was a deliberate, subjective choice by the decision-owners to set aside practical concerns and prioritise the quality of the experience. Rather than weakening the decision, this insight clarified the underlying values driving the choice and ultimately strengthened the case for the Okavango Delta as the more robust option.

Formalisation and Final Decision

With the decision confirmed as both aligned (the *right decision*) and justified (the *right reasons)*, the process moved to formalisation.

1. **Case for the Decision:** The AI synthesised all the outputs into a concise **Case for the Decision** document. This summary included the original goal, an overview of the validation process (including the critical challenge) and a summary of the benefits, costs and risks. This document was used to secure formal approval from Mike and Cathy.

2. **Final Decision:** Once approval was given, the AI produced the final official output: the **Final Decision**. This document was used to guide the next and final phase, **Decision Adoption**. It contained the rationale for the choice and highlighted key considerations for adopting the decision, such as the need for a specialist tour operator and mandatory medical evacuation insurance.

Process Insights

This validation phase demonstrates the value of using an AI as a critical partner. The AI's ability to systematically check for alignment and, more importantly, to challenge the human rationale, was key to building confidence. The process ensured the final decision was not only the preferred choice but also a robust, justifiable and clearly documented conclusion, providing a solid foundation for the final adoption phase.

Appendix 4c

Final Decision: 'Choosing the Holiday of a Lifetime'

1. The Final Decision & Approval

- **Final Decision:** The Okavango Delta Mokoro & Mobile Safari is selected as the 'Holiday of a Lifetime'.
- **Approved By:** Mike and Cathy.
- **Date of Approval:** 10 July 2025.

2. Decision Context

This decision is the result of a structured process to choose a two- to three-week adventurous journey focused on spectacular nature and wildlife.

Six destinations were evaluated against eight differentiators:

- Custom Amazon Basin Deep Dive
- The Pantanal Wetlands & Wildlife Safari
- Costa Rica Rainforest & Cloud Forest Eco-Journey
- Namibian Wilderness & Skeleton Coast Expedition
- Okavango Delta Mokoro & Mobile Safari
- Bespoke Madagascar Biodiversity Quest

3. Rationale for Selection

The Okavango Delta was selected as the definitive winner following a rigorous evaluation, including 'what-if' analysis. The key reasons for its selection are:

- **Exceptional Wildlife Experience:** The primary driver for the decision was the Okavango Delta's 'Exceptional' rating for the 'Wow-Factor' of its wildlife. It offers one of the greatest concentrations of wildlife in Africa, including the 'Big 5' and a high density of predators, providing an unparalleled big-game safari experience.

- **Unique Combination of Adventure:** The proposed trip combines the dynamic, expeditionary adventure of a 4x4 mobile safari with the serene, intimate, and unique water-based exploration in a traditional mokoro canoe.

- **Strategic Trade-Off:** The decision explicitly accepts that this option is the most expensive of the finalists. This higher cost is embraced in exchange for a more exclusive, remote, and high-quality wildlife experience, which aligns with the core 'Holiday of a Lifetime' goal.

4. Key Considerations for Decision Adoption

As you move into the adoption phase (planning and booking), the following points from the research and validation are key:

- **Primary Stakeholders:** Mike and Cathy (Decision Owners).

- **Implementation Strategy:** The very high logistical complexity means that implementation will require engaging a specialist and reputable tour operator. They will be essential for managing the necessary light aircraft transfers, ground transport, and camp logistics.

- **Key Risks & Governance:**
  - **Health:** There is a significant malaria risk in the Okavango Delta. A consultation with a GP or travel clinic to discuss prophylaxis is a critical next step.

  - **Safety:** Due to the minimal medical facilities in the remote camps, obtaining comprehensive travel insurance that includes robust emergency medical evacuation coverage is mandatory.

Appendix 5a

Note: This super-prompt is also available to download from goalatlas. com/ai-augmented-decisions via the QR code below.

Decision Adoption Super-prompt

Instruction: Your role

In this conversation, you will play the role of an expert in the processes of decision-making. Your job is to guide the person prompting you through a structured, systematic approach to making a particular high-impact, high-complexity decision. The decision-making process comprises five phases, which together are designed to progressively refine thinking from a broad exploration of possibilities to a specific decision, while maintaining the option to revisit earlier phases of the process when necessary.

Your expertise in decision-making has been compiled into five super-prompts covering the five phases of high-impact, high-complexity decision-making. This document is the fifth and final 'super-prompt' covering the final phase of AI-augmented decisions: **Decision Adoption**.

The entire premise of AI-augmented decisions is that we end up with 'faster, smarter, better' decisions. Your role is to act as an adoption partner, helping to translate the final decision into a practical, human-centric and agile framework for action. Keep your suggestions concise and your questions simple. Keep asking whether the person prompting you wants to keep digging deeper into the topic you are currently focused on or move on to the next topic.

Context: AI-augmented decisions: an overview of the process

The five phases of the decision-making process are:

1. **Decision Scoping** - Defining what decision needs to be made and why.

2. **Decision Preparation** - Building the knowledge base for informed decision-making.

3. **Decision-Making Workshop** - Collaboratively evaluating options and reaching a proposed decision.

4. **Decision Validation** - Testing and challenging the decision before commitment.

5. **Decision Adoption** - Rolling out and implementing the decision.

Context: Where to apply this five-phase decision process

This process is designed specifically for high-impact, high-complexity decisions where:

- The stakes are significant for the organisation;

- Multiple factors and variables interact in complex ways;

- There are no clear 'right' answers, only better or worse choices;

- Implementation will require coordination across different parts of the organisation.

The process is particularly powerful for augmenting decisions about strategy and strategic planning, as well as innovation and transformation.

Context: Key design principles of the entire process

The process incorporates several important design principles:

1. **Divergent and convergent thinking:** All five phases include both divergent thinking (exploring broadly) and convergent thinking (narrowing focus).

2. **Iterative approach:** While the process moves generally from phase to phase, it allows for looping back to earlier phases when new insights require revising previous work.

3. **Complexity-aware:** The framework acknowledges that complex decisions involve emergent patterns, non-linear relationships and the

need for adaptation rather than rigid planning.

4. **Human-AI collaboration:** Throughout the process, human judgment and AI capabilities work together, with AI augmenting rather than replacing human decision-making.

Instruction: Preliminaries

The chat that you, the AI, are about to have with the person prompting you will be guided by the outputs from the previous phases. Before you begin, check that you have access to the **Final Decision** (from Phase 4: **Decision Validation**). This document is the primary input for the **Decision Adoption** phase and should contain:

- The final, validated decision statement and the rationale for its selection.

- Key considerations for adoption and implementation, which may include initial thoughts on stakeholders, strategy, risks and governance.

If you do not have this material, ask the person prompting you for it.

Once you have all you need, check that you have a sufficient understanding of the process you are being asked to augment. If you feel there are omissions or ambiguities, seek clarification sparingly. Once ready, say so.

By way of introduction, explain to the person prompting you that this is the fifth and final phase of AI-human collaboration. This phase, **Decision Adoption**, is about turning the final decision into action. It focuses on engaging people and creating an agile framework for **Decision Adoption**. It involves four key activities:

1. Producing a Checklist of Adoption Activities;

2. Identifying Key Stakeholders;

3. Establishing a Governance Framework;

4. Producing a pack of Decision Adoption Resources.

IMPORTANT: For some decisions, the adoption process will be elaborate and lengthy. For others it will be compact and brief. Always try to stick to the principle that AI-augmented decisions are **faster, smarter, better** decisions and hence make this **Decision Adoption** process only as complicated as the decision requires it to be. The detailed instructions below are primarily to give structure to an elaborate and lengthy **Decision Adoption** process and they may be truncated for a simpler process. You can even adapt the titles of the activities if they seem too formal for a simpler adoption process.

Context: Overview of the Decision Adoption process

This final phase is deliberately called **Decision Adoption**, not 'decision implementation'. Implementation can suggest a top-down, mechanical process of executing a master plan that is imposed from above. Adoption, by contrast, is a human-centric process focused on how people engage with a decision, commit to it and actively adapt their own work in response. It bridges the gap between deciding and doing - mobilising the right people, with the right resources, at the right time to realise the benefits of having made the decision.

The importance of this phase cannot be overstated. Without systematic adoption, decisions often remain as abstract intentions rather than concrete changes. They can be misinterpreted, diluted or even quietly abandoned as organisational attention shifts to other priorities. Effective adoption creates commitment across diverse stakeholder groups, ensures consistent understanding of what needs to happen and establishes the mechanisms needed for adoption activities to be successful.

At its core, **Decision Adoption** is fundamentally about securing the engagement and commitment of people. This human-centred reality makes **Decision Adoption** both more challenging and more nuanced than earlier phases of the decision journey. It needs to be a process with agility at its heart.

Decision Adoption is, therefore, a human-centric process focused on how people engage with, commit to, and adapt their work in response to the decision. It translates a **Final Decision** into a practical framework for action. The process consists of four activities:

Activity #1 – Producing a Checklist of Adoption Activities: The objective here is to identify, and prioritise, the different 'adoption activities' that need to come together for the **Final Decision** to be successfully adopted.

Activity #2 – Identifying Key Stakeholders: Once a **Checklist of Adoption Activities** has been recorded, the key people who will be involved in each of the activities need to be mapped onto the checklist, including those who drive decision adoption, those who will play an enabling role and those who will be significantly affected.

Activity #3 – Establishing a Governance Framework: This activity produces a **Governance Framework** that defines how progress will be tracked, how challenges will be addressed and how activities can be adapted in a controlled manner as new information emerges.

Activity #4 – Producing a pack of Decision Adoption Resources: The final activity of the process is to consolidate the outputs of the previous activities into a pack of **Decision Adoption Resources** that represent the ultimate intention of the decision and the best possible path forward based on the information known at this stage.

Instruction: Activity #1 - Producing a Checklist of Adoption Activities

Explain to the person prompting you that the first activity is to identify and prioritise the key 'adoption activities' required, i.e. all the things that need to be done for the decision to be successfully adopted.

Suggest an initial list of adoption activities, derived from information in the **Final Decision** and seek input from the person prompting you to revise and refine your suggestions.

Remind the person prompting you that the aim is to produce a **Checklist of Adoption Activities** (often referred to as a 'backlog' in agile processes). This is not intended to be a final, exhaustive script for the entirety of the adoption process, but rather an initial, prioritised list of activities, based on what we know now. It is understood from the outset that this is a dynamic list that will evolve as the adoption process unfolds. The initial list provides the starting point for the individuals and teams who will pull work from the top of this checklist to execute in short, iterative cycles or sprints.

Help the person prompting you to prioritise the **Checklist of Adoption Activities.**

Instruction: Activity #2 – Identifying key stakeholders

Once this checklist is taking shape, ask the person prompting you to start assigning people to the activities. If, at any stage, the person prompting you seems to be struggling to do so, suggest that each activity may need individuals or teams assigned to the following roles:

- **Decision Owners** – they have the formal authority to commit the organisation to the decision and with ultimate accountability for that decision and its outcomes. Decision Owners are key to **Decision Adoption** as they visibly advocate for the decision and remove organisational barriers to adoption. They provide the authority and resources needed for **Decision Adoption** while modelling commitment through their own actions and communications.

- **Managers and team leaders** with direct responsibility for executing specific aspects of the decision. These individuals translate high-level direction into operational plans, allocate resources within their areas of responsibility and manage day-to-day adoption activities.

- **Front-line staff / teams** who will change their daily work practices as a result of the decision. Their engagement is critical as they ultimately determine whether a decision becomes reality through countless small actions and choices.

- **Enabling Partners** – Technical specialists, support functions and subject matter experts who provide essential capabilities for successful **Decision Adoption**. These might include IT teams, HR professionals, financial analysts or external consultants.

- **Affected Stakeholders** – Groups who will experience the impact of the decision but may not be directly involved in its adoption. These could include customers, suppliers, community members or employees in adjacent functions.

Remind the person prompting you that the key to successful adoption is to get all stakeholders engaged and committed to the decision. Offer suggestions on what information they would need for:

- **Contextual understanding** – Helping each stakeholder group understand not just what needs to be done, but why it matters. How the decision connects to organisational purpose should be clearly and concisely communicated by explaining the evidence that informed the decision and demonstrating how **Decision Adoption** supports both organisational and individual success. Ideally, different information will be presented to different stakeholders in different ways at different times. Communications should be customised to the needs of different stakeholders and their involvement in the adoption process. Some stakeholders, for example, will need to understand, in depth, the challenge that necessitated the decision, the process by which the decision was reached, the details of what is encompassed by the decision and what remains to be decided by the decision adopters. Others will need a simple concise statement of the decision and an explanation of how their ways of working will need to adapt to support **Decision Adoption**.

- **Active participation** – Creating appropriate opportunities for stakeholders to shape **Decision Adoption** approaches. This might include involvement in detailed planning, participation in pilot initiatives or opportunities to provide feedback that influence how the decision is adopted.

- **Capability development** – Ensuring stakeholders have the skills, knowledge and resources needed for effective **Decision Adoption**. This includes training programs, decision support tools and access to expertise that builds confidence and competence.

- **Progress visibility** – Establishing mechanisms that allow stakeholders to see how their efforts contribute to overall adoption success. Regular updates, progress metrics and celebration of milestones help maintain momentum and reinforce commitment.

- **Feedback channels** – Creating safe, efficient ways for stakeholders to raise concerns, suggest improvements and highlight emerging issues. These channels ensure adoption can adapt to practical realities while maintaining alignment with strategic intent.

Seek feedback from the person prompting you to revise and refine your suggestions on the best way to provide information to stakeholders to secure their engagement and commitment to **Decision Adoption**.

Instruction: Activity #3 - Establishing a Governance Framework

Explain that this activity defines the 'rules of the game' for managing the adoption process in an agile way, ensuring it can adapt without losing direction. Offer to help the user define the key components of this **Governance Framework**.

Guide the person prompting you through the following questions, offering suggestions and asking for their input:

- How can we set **Success Metrics** to provide a balanced view of both adoption activities (progress measures) and resulting outcomes (impact measures)?

- Do we schedule **Iterative Adoption Cycles (Sprints)**? Rather than long review periods, adoption is managed in short, time-boxed cycles (e.g., two-to-four-week sprints). At the end of each sprint, a review is held to demonstrate progress, gather feedback, and adapt the checklist for the next cycle.

- How do we establish **Escalation Pathways** that enable quick resolution of obstacles that threaten the success of decision adoption?

- How do we design **Learning Systems** that capture insights from **Decision Adoption** experience to refine approaches and build organisational capability?

- How do we manage **Transition Planning** that establishes how temporary **Decision Adoption** structures will eventually give way to sustainable operations once the decision is fully adopted?

Once these questions are defined, summarise them concisely in the form of a **Governance Framework**.

Instruction: Activity #4 - Producing the Decision Adoption Resources

Explain that the final activity is to consolidate all the outputs from this entire phase into a single, comprehensive pack of **Decision Adoption Resources**. Remind the user that this is a living set of documents, intended to guide and evolve, not a rigid blueprint.

Offer to draft the pack by compiling the outputs from the previous activities and documents. Explain that a robust pack of **Decision Adoption Resources** typically includes:

- The **Final Decision** document;
- **Checklist of Adoption Activities** (mapped to relevant stakeholders);
- **Governance Framework**.

Remind the person prompting you that this resource pack is the organisation's formal commitment to move from deciding to action. It transforms the rigour of the preceding decision-making process into a tangible, manageable and measurable way of working. Present the draft **Decision Adoption Resources** to the person prompting you for review and refinement. Once they are happy with them, present the final pack of **Decision Adoption Resources** in a form suitable to download or copy-and-save.

Instruction: Concluding the AI-Augmented Decision Process

Advise the person prompting you that the five-phase AI-augmented decisions process is now complete. The focus now shifts from deciding to doing. The **Decision Adoption Resources** provide the strategic foundation and operational framework for a journey of iterative execution, learning and adaptation. The organisation is now equipped not just with a high-quality decision, but with a clear and actionable path to turning that decision into meaningful and lasting change.

Appendix 5b

Summary of Decision Adoption: 'Choosing the Holiday of a Lifetime'

AI platform: https://gemini.google.com (version 2.5 Pro)
Date of chat: 10 July 2025
Documents uploaded:

- Decision Adoption Super-prompt

- Final Decision (Holiday of a Lifetime)

This case study demonstrates the AI-augmented **Decision Adoption** phase, conducted in a conversation with Google Gemini. Following the formal selection of the Okavango Delta Mokoro & Mobile Safari, the objective of this final phase was to translate the decision into a concrete and actionable plan. This phase focuses on the human-centric process of engaging with the decision to ensure it moves from an abstract intention to a tangible reality.

A full transcript of the entire conversation can be found online at goalatlas. com/ai-augmented-decisions via the QR code below.

The process involved four key activities.

1. Producing a Checklist of Adoption Activities

The first activity was to create a prioritised checklist of the actions required to make the holiday happen. The AI's initial suggestions were refined through a collaborative conversation. The user pointed out that finalising dates should not be the first step, but rather the result of an initial exploration of trade-offs between factors like climate, cost and tourist density. This critical human insight led to a more realistic and savvy plan. The final output was a three-step 'Sequence of Planning Activities':

- **Step 1: Exploration, Viability & Quotation:** This involved exploring a range of dates to analyse trade-offs, selecting a specialist tour operator, getting a firm quote and consulting a travel clinic.

- **Step 2: Booking & Commitment:** This step covered the final go/no-go decision, followed by booking the safari package, flights and comprehensive insurance.

- **Step 3: Final Preparations:** This included finalising passports, visas, health plans and a packing list.

2. Identifying Key Stakeholders

With a clear action plan in place, the process moved to mapping the key people and partners required for its execution. For this personal decision, the stakeholders identified were:

- **Decision Owners:** Mike and Cathy, who are responsible for driving the entire planning process.

- **Enabling Partners:** External specialists including the Specialist Tour Operator, GP/Travel Clinic, Insurance Provider, and Airlines.

- **Affected Stakeholders:** Family, friends, or employers who needed to be informed of the travel dates.

3. Establishing a Governance Framework

This activity established simple 'rules of the game' to keep the planning process on track, agile and effective. Working with the AI, Mike and Cathy defined a concise framework:

- **Success Metrics:** To have the trip fully booked within two months and to keep the cost within the signed-off budget.

- **Rhythm & Process:** A quick check-in every Sunday evening to review progress and plan the week ahead.

- **Roadblock Resolution:** If disagreement or obstacles arose, the plan was to use the AI as a mediator by providing it with the relevant data and asking for an analysis of options against the original acceptance criteria.

- **Information Management:** A shared digital document would be used as a central repository for all research and booking confirmations.

4. Producing a Pack of Decision Adoption Resources

The final step consolidated these outputs into a single, comprehensive pack of **Decision Adoption Resources**. This living document provided the strategic foundation and operational plan to move from the final decision to the final execution.

Process Insights

This final phase highlighted the importance of translating a high-level decision into a practical, step-by-step plan. The AI served as an effective partner in structuring the adoption process, while the human user provided crucial real-world experience to refine and improve the AI's suggestions. This collaborative approach ensured the final plan was not only logical but also practical and grounded in experience, providing a clear and robust path to realising the 'Holiday of a Lifetime'.

Appendix 5c

Decision Adoption Resources: 'Choosing the Holiday of a Lifetime'

Date: 10 July 2025

1. The Final Decision & Rationale

- **Final Decision:** The Okavango Delta Mokoro & Mobile Safari is selected as the 'Holiday of a Lifetime'.
- **Decision Owners:** Mike and Cathy.
- **Approval Date:** 10 July 2025.
- **Core Rationale:** The Okavango Delta was chosen for three key reasons:
  - Exceptional Wildlife: It offers one of Africa's greatest wildlife concentrations and an unparalleled big-game safari experience, which was the primary driver for the decision.
  - Unique Adventure: The trip uniquely combines an expeditionary 4x4 mobile safari with serene, water-based exploration in a traditional mokoro canoe.
  - Strategic Trade-Off: A higher cost is consciously accepted in exchange for a more exclusive, remote, and high-quality wildlife experience that aligns with the core 'Holiday of a Lifetime' goal.

2. Sequence of Planning Activities & Stakeholders

Step 1: Exploration, Viability & Quotation

- **Actions:**
  - Explore a range of potential travel dates, analysing trade-offs (climate, cost, crowds).
  - Finalise the optimal travel dates based on the analysis.
  - Select a specialist tour operator and get a detailed itinerary and firm quote.

- Consult a GP/travel clinic regarding health requirements (malaria, etc.).
- **Stakeholders Involved:** Mike & Cathy, Specialist Tour Operator(s), Airlines, GP/Travel Clinic.

Step 2: Booking & Commitment

- **Actions:**
    - Make the final go/no-go decision based on Step 1.
    - Book the complete safari package.
    - Book international flights.
    - Obtain comprehensive travel insurance, including mandatory emergency medical evacuation coverage.
- **Stakeholders Involved:** Mike & Cathy, Chosen Tour Operator, Airline, Insurance Provider.

Step 3: Final Preparations

- **Actions:**
    - Ensure passports are valid for the required duration.
    - Arrange any necessary visas.
    - Execute the health plan (vaccinations, prescriptions).
    - Develop and finalise a packing list.
- **Stakeholders Involved:** Mike & Cathy. Inform any Affected Stakeholders (e.g., family, employers).

3. Our Planning Framework

Success Metrics:

- **Progress:** Have the trip fully booked within two months.
- **Impact:** Keep the total cost within the signed-off budget estimates.

Rhythm & Process:

- We will have a quick check-in every Sunday evening to review progress and plan the next week's tasks.

Roadblock Resolution:

- If we get stuck or disagree, we will prompt our AI with the challenge, provide all relevant data, and ask for the pros and cons of our options in relation to our agreed criteria.

Information Management:

- We will use a shared digital document to act as a central repository for all research, quotes, links, and booking confirmations.

With the completion of this pack, the five-phase AI-augmented decisions process is now complete.

The focus now shifts from *deciding* to *doing*. The **Decision Adoption Resources** we have just created provide the strategic foundation and operational framework for your journey of execution, learning, and adaptation. You are now equipped not just with a high-quality decision, but with a clear and actionable path to turning that decision into a meaningful and lasting change - in this case, the 'Holiday of a Lifetime'.

I wish you the very best with your planning and an incredible trip to the Okavango Delta.

References

All online sources accessed between December 2024 and August 2025.

[1] National Cyber-Security Centre, May 2025. *AI Data Security - Best Practices for Securing Data Used to Train & Operate AI Systems.* https://media.defense.gov/2025/May/22/2003720601/-1/-1/0/CSI_AI_DATA_SECURITY.PDF

[2] Information Commissioner's Office, 2025. *Guidance on AI and data protection.* https://ico.org.uk/for-organisations/uk-gdpr-guidance-and-resources/artificial-intelligence/guidance-on-ai-and-data-protection/

[3] https://goalatlas.com/

[4] Perplexity.ai 2025. Prompt: *'Is there evidence that organisations are making decisions in circumstances of greater complexity than they did previously?'* 14-step analysis, 30 sources, March 2025. https://www.perplexity.ai/search/is-there-evidence-that-organis-rZxX1cn7S6mKYNNyIcGMtQ

[5] Perplexity.ai 2025. Prompt: *'Is there evidence that organisations need to make decisions faster than they previously needed to?'* 10-step analysis, 54 sources, March 2025. https://www.perplexity.ai/search/is-there-evidence-that-organis-YtL12lxLSmGlao3Fdi1eow

[6] Perplexity.ai 2025. Prompt: *'I want to propose that a process for making faster, smarter, better decisions, based on decision science, complexity theory and behavioural economics would comprise the following five phases 1. Decision brief, 2. Decision preparation, 3. Decision making, 4. Decision validation and 5. Decision adoption. To what extent is this supported by research?'* 17-step analysis, 52 sources, March 2025. https://www.perplexity.ai/search/i-want-to-propose-that-a-proce-d1MdSaEMSmSz8vSd7VUnSw

[7] Learn more about Mike's work at https://goalatlas.com/about-us/

[8] Wikipedia, 2025. *Margaret Boden.* https://en.wikipedia.org/wiki/Margaret_Boden

[9] Such as Ometria https://ometria.com

[10] Google Gemini Deep Research, July 2025. *The Dual Frontiers of AI in Late 2024: Juggernaut Models and Hyper-Efficient Competitors.* Prompt and response saved at https://docs.google.com/document/d/1J7i8axpsFJKmFqoHf4Gyt1IH9f74MI4ZwhKuSeohxLg/edit?usp=sharing

[11] Wikipedia, 2025. *Generative pre-trained transformer.* https://en.wikipedia.org/wiki/Generative_pre-trained_transformer

[12] Google Gemini Deep Research, July 2025. *An Analysis of Transparency in Custom GPTs and Large Language Models.* Prompt and response saved at https://docs.

google.com/document/d/1j5M6RLp28J5PY8Tdf9E6tmBrk-vmFom9iUQ-zMpC_DI/edit?usp=sharing

[13] OpenAI's GPT Store. https://chatgpt.com/gpts

[14] Baxter MR, 2020. *The Strategy Manual: A step-by-step guide to the transformational change of anything.* Goal Atlas, London.

[15] Baxter MR, 2023. *Core Values... and how they underpin strategy & organisational culture.* Goal Atlas, London.

[16] Wikipedia, 2025. *Foundation model.* https://en.wikipedia.org/wiki/Foundation_model

[17] Gary Marcus, 2024. *LLMs don't do formal reasoning - and that is a HUGE problem.* https://garymarcus.substack.com/p/llms-dont-do-formal-reasoning-and

[18] A good overview of the idea of deep research, as related to Generative AI platforms, is at https://openai.com/index/introducing-deep-research/

[19] Gemini Deep Research, 2025. https://gemini.google/overview/deep-research/?hl=en

[20] Perplexity.ai, 2025. *Getting Started.* https://www.perplexity.ai/hub/getting-started

[21] Baxter M and Baxter S, 2024. *Deep Design Thinking.* Goal Atlas, London.

[22] Baxter MR, 2020. *The Strategy Manual: A step-by-step guide to the transformational change of anything.* Goal Atlas, London.

[23] Perplexity.ai, 2025. Prompt: *'Is there compelling evidence that the lifespan of organisation has been getting shorter over recent decades? I seem to recall that the time companies spend in top performance leagues, such as the S&P 500 or FTSE 100 has been falling over maybe the past 100 years. Look for any evidence of company lifespan changes or changes in duration of top performance'.* 28-step analysis, 38 sources, March 2025. https://www.perplexity.ai/search/is-there-compelling-evidence-t-3zdCM.bzTqudsiy4O_axsg

[24] Wikipedia, 2025. *Steven Sasson: First self-contained digital camera.* https://en.wikipedia.org/wiki/Steven_Sasson#First_self-contained_digital_camera

[25] Vinokuruva N and Kapoor R, 2023. *Kodak's Surprisingly Long Journey Towards Strategic Renewal: A Half Century of Exploring Digital Transformation that Culminated in Failure.* Wharton School Research Paper. http://dx.doi.org/10.2139/ssrn.4373683

[26] Kmia O, 2022. *Why Kodak Died and Fujifilm Thrived: A Tale of Two Film Companies.* https://petapixel.com/why-kodak-died-and-fujifilm-thrived-a-tale-of-two-film-companies/

[27] The Economist, 2012. *The last Kodak moment?* https://www.economist.com/node/21542796

[28] Wikipedia, 2025. *Groupthink.* https://en.wikipedia.org/wiki/Groupthink

[29] Adrian Segar, 2021. *The danger of our drive to make sense.* https://www.conferencesthatwork.com/index.php/learning/2021/01/our-drive-to-make-sense/

[30] Khachadourian V (no date) *Commentary by Enough Trace on Oracle's 2023 Decision Dilemma Report with full copy of report attached.* https://www.enoughtrace.com/enough_trace_dot_com_data/no_clicks/decision_dilemma_global_study_Oracle_Apr2023.pdf

[31] Brookes W, 2023. *The new landscape of collaborative purchasing decision-making.* https://www.warc.com/newsandopinion/opinion/the-new-landscape-of-collaborative-purchasing-decision-making/en-gb/6111

[32] Zylo, 2023. *Too Many Apps? When More Becomes Too Much.* https://zylo.com/blog/too-many-apps/

[33] Lucid, 2023. *The Real Impact of Business Complexity.* https://lucid.co/blog/business-complexity

[34] Rittel HWJ and Webber MM, 1973. Dilemmas in a General Theory of Planning. *Policy Sciences* 4: 155-169. https://doi.org/10.1007/BF01405730

[35] Perplexity.ai, 2025. Prompt: *'What are the key differences between complicated and complex problems'.* 9 sources, April 2025. https://www.perplexity.ai/search/what-are-the-key-differences-b-jA7UND2lT2qlAKHEc67.Yw

[36] My research on design thinking was first published in Baxter MR, 1995. *Product Design: Practical Methods for the Systematic Development of New Products.* Chapman Hall, London and has recently been extended in Baxter MR and Baxter SH, 2024. *Deep Design Thinking.* Goal Atlas, London.

[37] Baxter MR, 2020. *The Strategy Manual: A step-by-step guide to the transformational change of anything.* Goal Atlas, London.

[38] Perplexity.ai, 2025. Prompt: *'I want to propose that a process for making faster, smarter, better decisions, based on decision science, complexity theory and behavioural economics would comprise the following five phases 1. Decision brief, 2. Decision preparation, 3. Decision making, 4. Decision validation and 5. Decision adoption. To what extent is this supported by research'* 17-step analysis, 52 sources, March 2025. https://www.perplexity.ai/search/i-want-to-propose-that-a-proce-d1MdSaEMSmSz8vSd7VUnSw

[39] Baxter MR, 2020. *The Strategy Manual: A step-by-step guide to the transformational change of anything.* Goal Atlas, London, p230.

[40] Baxter M and Baxter S, 2024. *Deep Design Thinking.* Goal Atlas Ltd, London.

Divergent and convergent thinking are defined on p21. The section on divergent and convergent thinking as a defining characteristic of design thinking is on p27.

41 Wikipedia, 2025. *Generative artificial intelligence.* https://en.wikipedia.org/wiki/Generative_artificial_intelligence

42 Wikipedia, 2025. *AI winter: Slowdown in deployment of expert systems.* https://en.wikipedia.org/wiki/AI_winter#Slowdown_in_deployment_of_expert_systems

43 Hacker News, 2021. *Rules Based Expert Systems.* https://news.ycombinator.com/item?id=29439117

44 Wikipedia, 2025. *Artificial intelligence.* https://en.wikipedia.org/wiki/Artificial_intelligence

45 Red Hat, 2024. *What is an AI platform?* https://www.redhat.com/en/topics/ai/what-is-an-ai-platform

46 Google Cloud, 2024 The Prompt: *'What is long context — and why does it matter for your AI?'* https://cloud.google.com/transform/the-prompt-what-are-long-context-windows-and-why-do-they-matter

47 Wikipedia, 2025. *Generative artificial intelligence.* https://en.wikipedia.org/wiki/Generative_artificial_intelligence

48 Red Hat, 2024. *Predictive AI vs. generative AI.* https://www.redhat.com/en/topics/ai/predictive-ai-vs-generative-ai

49 Wikipedia, 2025. *Large language model.* https://en.wikipedia.org/wiki/Large_language_model

50 Wikipedia, 2025. *Machine learning.* https://en.wikipedia.org/wiki/Machine_learning

51 Google Cloud, 2025. *Prompt engineering: overview and guide.* https://cloud.google.com/discover/what-is-prompt-engineering?hl=en

52 Hawkins B, 2024. *Super Prompt: What Is It and How to Write Your Own.* https://beginswithai.com/super-prompt-for-ai/

53 Ahzar M and Petrovic S, 2025. You've been prompting wrong this whole time. *Exponential View.* https://www.exponentialview.co/p/how-to-train-your-ai

54 Salvator D, 2025. *Explaining Tokens — the Language and Currency of AI.* https://blogs.nvidia.com/blog/ai-tokens-explained/

55 Perplexity.ai, 2025. Prompt: *'I am writing a book called AI-Augmented Decisions: A Practical Guide and I want to explain what capabilities modern consumer AIs, like Claude, ChatGPT and Gemini have recently acquired that make them able to usefully augment human decision-making. I'm thinking that these capabilities might include large context windows, chain-of-thought reasoning and nuanced language understanding/generation.*

Whilst I am focused on decision-making, it would be useful to know the capabilities modern AIs have to augment a wider range of sophisticated, knowledge-intensive human activities, such as writing, reasoning and problem solving-solving' 27-step analysis, 40 sources, April 2025. https://www.perplexity.ai/search/i-am-writing-a-book-called-ai-zzs4VK6VQ2e8v14DoO2GPA

[56] Jun Y, 2024. *Evaluating long context large language models.* https://www.artfish.ai/p/long-context-llms

[57] Wang J et al, 2024. *A Comprehensive Review of Multimodal Large Language Models: Performance and Challenges Across Different Tasks.* https://arxiv.org/html/2408.01319v1

[58] Gupta S et al, 2024. *A Comprehensive Survey of Retrieval-Augmented Generation (RAG): Evolution, Current Landscape and Future Directions.* https://arxiv.org/abs/2410.12837

[59] Wei J, 2022. *Chain-of-Thought Prompting Elicits Reasoning in Large Language Models.* https://arxiv.org/pdf/2201.11903

[60] Produced for this book, based on a conversation thread with ChatGPT 4o. The total information-processing speed of either a biological or electronic system will be determined by 1. its signal generation speed, 2. its signal transmission speed and 3. its signal switching speed.
Sources for 1. Neuron Firing Rate vs. CPU Cycle Speed: Neurons fire at ~200 Hz: Dayan P and Abbott LF, 2001. *Theoretical Neuroscience: Computational and Mathematical Modeling of Neural Systems.* Cambridge, MA: MIT Press and Purves, D et al, 2018. *Neuroscience.* 6th ed. Sunderland, MA: Sinauer Associates. CPUs operate at ~1–4 GHz: Intel Corporation, 2024. *Processor Base Frequency Specifications.* [online] Available at: https://ark.intel.com. Speedup Estimate: ~10 million times.
Sources for 2. Axon Signal Transmission vs. Electronic Signal Speed: Myelinated axons transmit at ~120 m/s: Kandel ER, Schwartz JH, Jessell TM, Siegelbaum SA and Hudspeth AJ, 2013. *Principles of Neural Science.* 5th ed. New York: McGraw-Hill. Electronics transmission ~300,000,000 m/s: Horowitz M et al, 2014. *Computing's energy problem (and what we can do about it).* IEEE Spectrum, 51(2), pp.29–35. Speedup Estimate: ~2.5 million times.
Sources for 3. Ionic Synapse Response vs. Transistor Switching. Ion channels take ~1–5 ms: Hille B, 2001. *Ion Channels of Excitable Membranes.* 3rd ed. Sunderland, MA: Sinauer Associates. Transistors switch in ~1 ps Bohr MT and Young IA, 2009. *CMOS scaling trends and beyond.* IEEE Micro, 29(4), pp.20–29. Speedup Estimate: ~1 billion times.

[61] ChatGPT, 2025. https://chatgpt.com/

[62] Google's Gemini, 2025. https://gemini.google.com/

[63] Anthropic's Claude, 2025. https://claude.ai/

[64] xAI's Grok, 2025. https://grok.com/chat

[65] DeepSeek, 2025. https://chat.deepseek.com/

[66] Andrej Karpathy, 2025. https://x.com/karpathy/status/1937902205765607626

[67] Mei L et al, 2025. *A Survey of Context Engineering for Large Language Models.* https://arxiv.org/pdf/2507.13334

[68] elder-plinius, 2025. *Anthropic Claude System Prompt.* https://github.com/elder-plinius/CL4R1T4S/blob/main/ANTHROPIC/Claude_4.txt

[69] Gemini Apps Privacy Hub, 2025. https://support.google.com/gemini/answer/13594961 (page updated June 11, 2025)

[70] Google Cloud, 2025. *Mastering secure AI on Google Cloud, a practical guide for enterprises.* https://cloud.google.com/blog/products/identity-security/mastering-secure-ai-on-google-cloud-a-practical-guide-for-enterprises

[71] National Cyber-Security Centre, May 2025. *AI Data Security - Best Practices for Securing Data Used to Train & Operate AI Systems.* https://media.defense.gov/2025/May/22/2003720601/-1/-1/0/CSI_AI_DATA_SECURITY.PDF

[72] Information Commissioner's Office, 2025. *Guidance on AI and data protection.* https://ico.org.uk/for-organisations/uk-gdpr-guidance-and-resources/artificial-intelligence/guidance-on-ai-and-data-protection/

[73] The Neuron, 2025. *How to run a local AI model on your computer with LM Studio.* https://www.theneuron.ai/explainer-articles/how-to-run-a-local-ai-model-on-your-computer-with-lm-studio

[74] Claude Sonnet 4, 2025. https://www.anthropic.com/claude/sonnet

[75] Perplexity.ai, 2025. *Introducing Perplexity Deep Research.* https://www.perplexity.ai/hub/blog/introducing-perplexity-deep-research

[76] Perplexity.ai, 2025. https://www.perplexity.ai/

[77] Chatbot App GPT-4o, April 2025. https://chat.chatbotapp.ai/gpt4o

[78] Gemini 2.5 Pro, 2025. https://deepmind.google/technologies/gemini/pro/

[79] NotebookLM, 2025. https://notebooklm.google.com/

[80] Hawkins B, 2024. *Super Prompt: What Is It and How to Write Your Own.* https://beginswithai.com/super-prompt-for-ai/

[81] Creative Commons, 2025. *Attribution 4.0 International.* https://creativecommons.org/licenses/by/4.0/

[82] OpenAI, 2025. *Memory FAQ: Learn more about managing memory in ChatGPT.* https://help.openai.com/en/articles/8590148-memory-faq

[83] Foy P, 2024. *Understanding Tokens & Context Windows.* https://blog.mlq.ai/tokens-context-window-llms/

[84] OpenAI, 2025. *What are tokens and how to count them?* https://help.openai.com/en/articles/4936856-what-are-tokens-and-how-to-count-them

[85] Codingscape, 2025. *LLMs with largest context windows.* https://codingscape.com/blog/llms-with-largest-context-windows
GPT-5 context window data from https://platform.openai.com/docs/models/gpt-5-chat-latest

[86] The Quoted Company Alliance, 2025. *Annual reports have become 'epic novels' as UK companies face growing reporting burden.* https://www.theqca.com/press-releases/annual-reports-have-become-epic-novels-as-uk-companies-face-growing-reporting-burden/

[87] Stanford Encyclopedia of Philosophy, 2025. *Defeasible Reasoning.* https://plato.stanford.edu/entries/reasoning-defeasible/

[88] Gemini 2.5 Pro, 2025. https://deepmind.google/models/gemini/pro/

[89] Term first devised by Avinash Kaushik, see item #5 of Kaushik A, 2006. *Seven Steps to Creating a Data Driven Decision Making Culture.* https://www.kaushik.net/avinash/seven-steps-to-creating-a-data-driven-decision-making-culture/

[90] Gemini 2.5 Pro, August 2025. Prompt: *'Is there any evidence about the importance of making decisions in a carefully designed, well-facilitated workshop involving all the key individuals with authority to implement the decision and with accountability for its outcomes?'* In a review of 59 sources, three key advantages to using workshops for important organisational decisions were found from published research: i) collective ownership and commitment, ii) enhanced quality of the solution, iii) improved organisational health and agility. https://docs.google.com/document/d/1NCZuZLEqdim15KT8JLdZ9HxqhRBF48dSyzc9yAh9uIA/edit?tab=t.0

[91] Goal Atlas, 2025. Adapted from *The 'H' Model of Strategy Adoption and Rules for Strategy Adoption Conversations.* https://goalatlas.com/h-model-of-strategy-adoption/

[92] National Cyber-Security Centre, May 2025. *AI Data Security - Best Practices for Securing Data Used to Train & Operate AI Systems.* https://media.defense.gov/2025/May/22/2003720601/-1/-1/0/CSI_AI_DATA_SECURITY.PDF

[93] Information Commissioner's Office, 2025. *Guidance on AI and data protection.* https://ico.org.uk/for-organisations/uk-gdpr-guidance-and-resources/artificial-intelligence/guidance-on-ai-and-data-protection/

[94] Awork, 2025. *Glossary: Backlog.* https://www.awork.com/glossary/backlog

www.ingramcontent.com/pod-product-compliance
Lightning Source LLC
Chambersburg PA
CBHW081810200326
41597CB00023B/4216